C4 609016 00 DB

D0637036

# WAINWRIGHT
## Milltown to Mountain

# W R Mitchell

GREAT N-ORTHERN

For BOB AND PAULINE

| Newcastle Libraries & Information Service | |
| --- | --- |
| C4 609016 00 DB | |
| **Askews** | Apr-2010 |
| 920 WAI | £16.99 |
| | |

Great Northern Books
PO Box 213, Ilkley, LS29 9WS
www.greatnorthernbooks.co.uk

© WR Mitchell 2009

Every effort has been made to acknowledge correctly and contact the copyright holders of material in this book. Great Northern Books Ltd apologises for any unintentional errors or omissions, which should be notified to the publisher.

All rights reserved. No part of this book may be reproduced in any form or by any means without permission in writing from the publisher, except by a reviewer who may quote brief passages in a review.

ISBN: 978 1 905080 66 3

Design and layout: David Burrill

CIP Data
A catalogue for this book is available from the British Library

# Contents

# Prologue

Ilook back on my Wainwright years with joy and not a little emotion. The Lakeland fells, which I have known and loved for over half a century, took on a special character when, on a not-to-be-forgotten day in the 1950s, I was privileged to see the art work of AW's first pictorial guide before it was printed. As Editor of Cumbria for over thirty years, I got to know the man himself and his foibles.

I was quietly satisfied in 1992 – a year after his death – at being the author of After You, Mr Wainwright, the first of many books in which AW has been featured. That book was dedicated to Betty, his loving wife of thirty years. With an amused smile, she had accepted the presidency of a quartet of enthusiastic fellgoers – Bob, Stan, Colin and myself – who had formed the Geriatric Blunderers' Walking Club (motto: you name it, we've been lost on it).

Bob was already well-known to AW and Betty. In her later years, she revelled in reports about our high-level antics. Her presidency was by dint of providing us with afternoon tea at least once a year. When she had a stroke and her eyesight weakened, the reports sent to her were tape-recorded. In a letter dictated to one of her helpers but signed by her, in the springtime of 2005 – she added: "Thank you again for keeping me in touch. Love and all good wishes."

Thousands of AW's meticulous drawings of Lakeland fells have appeared in print elsewhere. This book takes a homely look at AW and the antics of the Blunderers. It has been written with the knowledge and approval of Betty's daughter Jane and with the much-appreciated help of Linda, AW's great niece.

*Alfred Wainwright in his upstairs study at Kendal works on one of his meticulous Lakeland drawings. (Photo: Westmorland Gazette)*

I have found the pen, in my hands, no instrument for
describing the captivating charms of Lakeland. It is
an emotion - and emotions are felt, not expressed.

*At the launch of "Fellwalking with Wainwright", 1984.*

*Chapter One*

# The Indomitable Mr Wainwright.

Alfred Wainwright (1907-91) bestrode the lonely fells of the Lake District, making notes and taking photographs. When I questioned his lonesome state on the fells, he admitted that to others his walks might seem erratic, leading to unfrequented corners. Yet his felltop zig-zags were to make Lakeland the raw material for an original idea in the making of books - a series of Pictorial Guides to the fells of the Lake District.

Each page – art work and text – would be hand-written, hand-drawn, free of printer's type. What he conceived simply as a record of walks to cheer him in old age, a time of wheezy lungs and wobbly legs, would become a publishing sensation. Wainwright, whose profession was accountancy, whose manner was quiet, taciturn and modest, became a national superstar.

I first knew him in the late 1950s, when he presided over the finance department at Kendal Town Hall. To his friends, he was AW. He did not care much for his Christian name, which was Alfred. He considered it was nice for a small boy but not very manly. My last glimpse of AW was when he and his wife Betty called to see me on the eve of my retirement from editorship of Cumbria magazine. By this time, he walked haltingly. Facially, he had what we in the north call "a good colour". Strands of grey hair over-lapped his coat collar. We had supported him when he needed additional publicity for his unique books. The first advert for them appeared in Cumbria in 1955.

AW was born in poverty, amid the clatter of textile machinery. Jobwise, he rose from office boy at the Town Hall in Blackburn to an exalted position at Kendal, where he was content to stay for the rest of his working life – close to his beloved Lakeland fells. Most of his spare time was spent on the highspots of Lakeland, his rucksack containing map, camera, notebook and pencil. He never mastered the art of using a compass. Pipe and tobacco were constant appendages, indoors or out.

Recording the routes he followed, and the natural features round about, brought method into his skyline excursions - and a compelling but demanding hobby for otherwise lonesome evenings.. He rejoiced when the Ordnance Survey re-published two-and-a-half inch maps that were satisfyingly rich in detail. Rough notes were quickly supplanted by distinctive Wainwright features – his own up-to-date maps, informative diagrams and immaculate drawings.

AW aimed for accuracy and attractiveness. To him, writing was a form of drawing. Drawings and diagrams occupied first place in his attention. With his "pictorial guides" he was on to something new. Work on Book One began, with only a cat for company, during an autumnal evening in 1952.

Rather more than two years later, that first book, dealing with the Eastern Fells, was completed. He had tidily fitted on to its 300 pages no less than 500 illustrations relating to the Helvellyn and Fairfield groups.

Domestically, pen and ink were as vital as knife and fork, except for fish and chips, a treat in his milltown childhood that remained a treat into old age. AW would produce many other pocketable guide books – and also a weighty tome, Westmorland Heritage, a labour of love that is also a supreme work of art. Published in 1974, when pretty little Westmorland was absorbed in the vast new county of Cumbria, the book runs to almost 500 pages.

To list AW's publishing achievements would invite writer's cramp. When he had covered Lakeland's principal fells, he produced a guide book to 102 outlying fells. He detailed walks in his beloved Limestone Country of North Craven, which he had trodden with his small son Peter. Lakeland received blanket coverage but he also visited – twice a year, for over 30 years, the Highlands and Islands of Scotland. He resisted the temptation to wear a kilt. AW presented, in what was now a recognised Wainwright form, a guide to the 250-mile Pennine Way, which at that time was the longest continuous footpath in the land. His most popular long distance walk would be the Coast to Coast – actually, a collection of walks, running against the grain of the north-country from St Bees to Robin Hoods Bay – a boot-warming 190 miles.

To me, Wainwright at his best – and that means his most inventive – was evident in a modest and little-known publication entitled Old Roads of Eastern Lakeland. In his Lakeland walks, he was ever-aware that wherever his feet trod someone had been there before him. Signs of human activity were everywhere evident on the maps he scrutinised. In this little book he dealt with "an intricate network of trodden ways and primitive roads" on the fells. "Every route had a definite objective, a definite purpose."

Over half a century has elapsed since AW came into my life. As mentioned, I was editing the magazine Cumbria, which was printed on the jobbing presses of the Gazette in Stricklandgate, Kendal. Harry Firth, the manager of that department, showed me the art work for Book One before this had been handed over to the printer. AW's grand scheme was launched in 1955 with a print run of 2,000 copies, retail price 12s.6d. He had persuaded an old friend, Henry Marshall, Librarian at Kendal, to deal with distribution and sales.

Initially, such was the novelty of the guide, sales were sufficient to defray almost half the printer's bill. All the copies had been sold by February. The printer's bill being

*Wainwright Country. He admired the fortitude of the hill sheep.*

settled, a reprint was ordered for Easter. Wainwright had arrived with a splosh if not with a bang. Untypically, but keen to tap a wider market, for the first time in his life he sought self-publicity.

That first advertisement in Cumbria was novel and unpretentious. Instead of a bold heading to set it off, there was a short message: "This is to announce the publication of a book that is quite out of the ordinary" being "primarily a book for fellwalkers – for those who know the fells intimately and for those who know them but little." Wainwright sensed that support would come from lovers of Lakeland and collectors of unusual books. Copies of the first in the series under the title of A Pictorial Guide to the Lakeland Fells were stated to be available at Lakeland bookshops or by post (for sixpence) from Henry Marshall, Low Bridge, Kentmere, Westmorland.

AW's fascination with the Lakeland highspots had begun when, in 1930, accompanied by a cousin named Eric Beardsall, he spent a week's holiday in the region. The climactic moment followed an ascent of Orrest Head. Into view came a shimmering Windermere and the dramatic Coniston Fells. To AW, a milltown lad, this was heaven on earth. Years later, when he obtained a post in the Borough Treasurer's office at Kendal, heaven was brought closer to hand.

AW was good at his accountancy and at his relations with his colleagues. His work was meticulous. His penmanship, in those pre-computer days, had style. AW had enjoyed writing and drawing since boyhood. His passion for fell-walking was the culmination of modest walks not far from home, including Pendle, a gloriously isolated hill, and the moors and dales of Bowland.

Now, at his Kendal home, an idea for producing hand-drawn guide books to the fells evolved into a spectacular reality. He was mountain-building on sheets of paper. Addressing himself, he said: "Let's do Great Gable as seen from Lingmell." The mountain he drew was as it was, not – as with many artists – in an imaginative or romantic style. His transport to the foot of the chosen fell was mainly a service bus. He would stay at a bed-and-breakfast establishment at a time when the cost was 4s a night. He walked in everyday clothes and had stout shoes on his feet, though he soon graduated to ex-army nailed boots.

When I first met him in his treasurer's office in Kendal Town Hall he told me that any profit from his guides would be allocated to Animal Rescue Cumbria, with Kapellan, a rescue centre, situated near Kendal. He described Kapellan as "a most beautiful place". It had been established, and was largely maintained, with money he received from his guides.

When, in 1988, he came to see me at my editorial office in Clapham, he was keen to talk about animal welfare, needing little encouragement. "When I walked the fells, animals were my only companions. They had an uncomplaining acceptable of the conditions in which they lived – out in dreadful weather all the time." He mentioned red deer, fell ponies and foxes. The bird life he encountered in Lakeland ranged from the spry wren that sang lustily on high crags to the lordly golden eagle, one of a pair, that circled high enough to take in a major part of Lakeland at a glance.

His appearance on the day he called, with Betty as his chauffeur, belied his 80 years. He continued to indulge his love for pipe-smoking. A few months before, he had been in the Scottish Highlands with the BBC, preparing films for a series to be screened that spring. He told me about his continually busy writing life, though sadly his eyesight had deteriorated to the extent that he could no longer read newspapers. "I use a typewriter as much by instinct as by sight."

He had further books in mind. And he retained the interest of Totty, his favourite among the eight erstwhile stray cats that shared the facilities at the Kendal home he occupied with Betty, the wife he adored.

*Chapter Two*

# Milltown poverty – A drunken father – Chapel days – A Town Hall job – Fish and chips.

AW's road to the high fells of Lakeland began, unpromisingly, at the busy industrialised town of Blackburn. He was born in a "two up, two down" terrace house. It was a time when poverty stalked the streets of the Lancashire milltowns. AW's milltown background was also mine. I was born and reared at Skipton, an outpost of the realm of King Cotton and at the northern edge of an industrialised zone where – 'twas said - crows flew backwards to keep flecks of soot out of their eyes.

Like AW, I grew up in straitened times. The mill chimneys were smokeless for long periods. In the cotton boom of Victorian times, a grandfather, seeking work, had left his natal area in the Piddle Valley of Dorset for Burnley. He took his religious faith, which was Primitive Methodism, to an area where Nonconformity thrived. Praising the Lord was not just a Sunday obligation. Chapel life, in various forms, enlivened a dull daily round.

AW's family attended Furthergate Congregational Church. By the time the Wainwrights came to Blackburn in 1901, the church was large and thriving. In a commemorative booklet written in 1934, the minister wrote: "Think not only of the Sunday services in church; remember also the Sunday school, the Morning school, the graded departments in the afternoon, the P.S.E. [pleasant Sunday evening]."

He continued: "Sunday is a day of full activity, and no one knows its value and influence...Then think of the week, of the blare of bugle and the beat of drum; of the Girls' Guild and Institute; of mothers' Teas; of the Endeavour Societies; of the Choir rendering faithful service, not only in the church worship, but also on many occasions at social events; of the Minstrels making merriment in many a good cause; of class parties; of Dramatic performances and operettas and Tennis tournaments; of Ramblers whose communing with nature is not at all the solemn event, but a very happy break in the week....[The list was exhaustive]."

Blackburn was revealed with clarity and a modicum of colour in Wakes Week. The mills closed down, the smog dispersed and a goodly number of townsfolk headed for

*Lancashire milltown with typical terrace housing.*

*Millworker wearing the customary shawl.*

*Commemorative blue plaque at 331 Audley Range -- birthplace of Alfred Wainwright.*

the Lancashire coastal resorts of Morecambe and Blackpool. When I first sought AW's birthplace, in 1993, I had been provided with a sketch map of Blackburn's main roads. Jack Fish, a nephew of Alfred Wainwright, spread himself over two A4 sheets, ingeniously marking in the traffic lights with red dots. It was not quite up to the standard established by AW, but it got me to within a quarter of a mile of my destination.

I had spoken to Jack over the phone, mentioning my ambition to visit the birthplace of AW, to which a commemorative blue plaque had been attached. The modest birthplace had also been included in a Town Trail. At the time of my visit, Jack Fish was about to do the unWainwrightish thing and fly to Canada. He told me: "Uncle Alfred's birthplace is on the Accrington side of the town." As Jack winged his way across the Atlantic, I scrutinised his map in my search for 331 Audley Range.

Beyond the Clitheroe by-pass lay a terrifying world of roundabouts, multi-signs and impetuous young horn-pipping motorists. I kept to the map as far as the Town Centre, whereupon I blundered in roughly the right direction. Guidance came from a handsome immigrant from the Indian sub-continent, also from an old age pensioner

*Albert Wainwright as a young man around 1890. AW's father was invariably known as 'Pop'.*

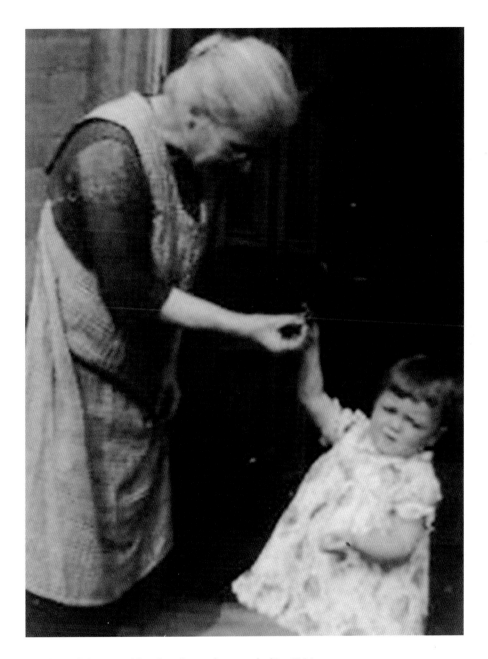

*Emily with her granddaughter Joan, photographed in 1931.*

*Opposite: Emily Woodcock (later Wainwright and AW's mother) standing at left, with her sisters Lucy (seated) and Annie. The photograph is thought to have been taken in Penistone around 1895.*

*Above: AW's sister Annie (left in both photographs) was a winder in a spinning mill.*

who'd never heard of Wainwright but knew a lot about Audley Range.

My last guide was a Council workman, who spoke when his pal was not being shaken to bits by a road drill. Eventually, standing beside a busy road, I had 331 Audley Range in view. It was a redbrick creation, cheek-by-jowl with others. The house had become something special. The blue plaque affixed to the front wall sported the Blackburn coat of arms and the words: "Alfred Wainwright/Author and Fell Walker (1907-1991)."

It was not easy to image AW as a baby, taking in his first lungful of air and mother's milk in a mean quarter of Edwardian Blackburn. This terrace was in a hilly situation that would have lifted it above the smog of Old Blackburn, though in AW's time it doubtless received smoke and muck from a nearby brickworks. His parents, Emily and Albert Wainwright, raised four children. Alice, the oldest, married John Fish and had two sons, Alan and Jack. Next in line was Frank, who spent some time in the Army.

Annie, who married Uncle Bill, was a winder in a spinning mill, producing the yarn that the weavers made into cloth. There was a strong tradition among the female mill-workers of being able to lip-read; the noise of the machinery made it impossible to hold a normal conversation. This affected their speech patterns and was evidenced in elderly women who moved their mouths in a slightly larger-than-life way and made the most of gestures for clarity and emphasis.

It was a time when a weaver – the proverbial "lassie from Lancashire" – operated several looms, collected weft from the store, carried pieces to the warehouse and, at the end of the day, swept and cleaned the machinery. A weaver wore a blouse and long skirt, over which was spread a "warkin' [working] brat [apron]". She was valued for her patience, her dexterity and speed.

The tools of her trade, held in a pouch, were a reed hook, comb and scissors. During the working day she moved incessantly, this way and that, attending to one loom that had become silent, then moving swiftly to another to correct a float [fault]. It was wise to correct it immediately. Such a blemish would be detected by the cut-looker when the cloth was examined in the warehouse.

Blackburn millworkers were no strangers to privation and poverty. Industrial and social changes produced a violent undercurrent, as proud artisans faced redundancy. In the bad old days, within the memory of AW and his family, "steaming" a shed kept the humidity high but created an unhealthy atmosphere for the workers. The Medical Officer of Health for Blackburn commented on this custom in 1887, and in the following year the borough's health committee instituted a special inquiry. It took a year to report – and not until 1929 was the problem of "steaming" tackled effectively and the recommendations received legal backing.

*Frank Wainwright (AW's brother), at far left, round about 1907.*
*The man operating the peepshow was 'owd chipper'.*

A mill worker lamented: "I'se nivver hed such a job i' mi life. If yer copped [caught] sweating, yer sacked." I met an old lady who, as a child coming home from school, recalled being greeted by her impoverished millworker mother with the words: "Here's a piece of bread, luv. Tak it round to your auntie and ask her to put some butter on't."

Alfred, the youngest of the Wainwright family, and hero of our story, was born in 1907 and grew up with a forest of smoking mill chimneys in the main part of town. A down-draught might suddenly blot out a few streets and induce a round of coughing. Alfred was to describe his natal home as a cottage which, in the Blackburn sense, was a term used for the poorest sort of workers' house.

A "cottage" was, nonetheless, an improvement on the constricted and common back-to-back. At the rear of the Wainwright house, a high wall shielded a vital milltown duo – privy and midden. There was no wash-house. Washing was done in th'back kitchen, where a coal-heated boiler stood in the corner by the slopstone [sink].

AW's birth occurred seven years and seven days after the birth of his sister, Annie Pretoria. However large he grew and however well-known he became, he was forever her little brother. Pretoria was a name that became topical in the Boer War. How it came to be used is related to Albert's heavy drinking.

When the family was living at Morecambe, Albert called at a pub on his way to register the birth of his third child. Having as usual stayed longer than was good for him – and his pocket – he thought it a good ideal to embellish the baby's name. He heard someone talking about the Boar War; they mentioned Pretoria. Albert had concluded that the town of Pretoria had been named after a lady!

Alice, his little sister, would recall AW's birth. She was about 12 years old when Father came into the children's bedroom one morning and said they had got another brother. "We all went into Mother's room to see what he was like...he seemed to me such a tiny baby. His eyes were dark and very shiny and his hair was light – the only one in our family with that colour, though Grandad was very sandy..."

Alfred, the baby of the family, sat at table for their meals – "he on a high chair with his back to the fire between Mother and Father. When I look back, I think: 'What a happy family we might have been if the cursed drink had never entered the home'." Father, a stonemason, once sober and upstanding, had become over-fond of alcohol and Emily, his wife, had a continually hard job "making ends meet". Daughter Alice wrote: "Mother had a smile and cheerful word for everyone she came in contact with and she helped many in trouble."

The house was rented at what to them was the princely sum of 4s.6d a week. Emily's unremitting domestic round included taking in washing and ironing from more affluent neighbours. AW, awakening at night, might heard the rumble of the mangle.

By taking in other people's washing, she was following an occupation common in the milltowns. Emily regularly cleaned other houses. Annie, her daughter, had a Saturday morning job, scrubbing the steps that led up to the Congregational minister's house. She hated it, but knew it was a way for the minister to supplement her mother's income without giving charity.

On my visit to Audley Range, a house-proud octogenarian who, having DIY fever, had just purchased a bag of cement, directed me to a house with a blue door. It was at that time the home of Sheila and Kenneth Dobson. Sheila, a niece of AW, was the daughter of Frank (a bricklayer known as Long Frank because of his height).

The Dobsons, who used to live at AW's birthplace, had never met Uncle Alfred but always intended to visit Kendal to rectify this. Kenneth's father, a watchmaker, hailed from Westmorland. Sheila's brother, Geoff, saw AW when, years before, he was visiting Blackburn to watch the Rovers play football. AW would call on Uncle Bill and Auntie Annie. Alan, the brother of Jack Fish, was said to be the "spit and image" of Uncle Alfred.

My quest for AW's connection with Blackburn had been set off by Mrs Lund (nee Helen Smith), first cousin of AW. She and her husband were living at High Bentham and were regular worshipers at the Methodist Chapel where, as a Methodist local preacher, I frequently took the services. Helen recalled that in her young days in Blackburn she had stayed with Auntie Emily (AW's mother) during summer holidays.

At dinnertime, a tall, red-haired lad (AW) would arrive for a meal. Married, with a young child, he lived in a new estate at the edge of town. Having an office job in the Town Hall, at lunchtime it was handy for him to drop in on his mother rather than go home. AW, with a Town Hall job, was earning 15 shillings a week.

Helen recalled: "He was pleasant enough but taciturn. He'd just say 'Hello' and 'Good-bye' and that was that." Perhaps his taciturnity arose as a response to the outpourings of his father who, when drunk, talked incessantly and would ask Alice to play the music for the hymn Lead, Kindly Light. Although they were poor, they did have a piano.

Auntie Emily (nee Woodcock) was much older than Helen's mother and was a member of a Penistone family consisting of twelve children. Emily's father had a large ironmonger's shop and, like her sisters, was expected to do jobs in the shop when not attending school. Emily's marriage to Albert Wainwright (AW's father) was solemnised in the Congregational Church at Penistone.

Helen recalled: "Aunt Emily was a saint if ever I knew one. She was of average build, with reddish cheeks – a lovely-looking person, though she was grey when I first knew her." Albert was from Millhouse near Penistone; he was a master mason, "charming when sober but garrulous and coarse when drunk." We have AW's own account of a hard, impoverished life at home and the antics of his often drunken father, who could not pass a public house without imbibing.

Helen recalled: "He was paid on a Friday. Annie Wainwright was sent to his favourite tippling place to demand some money or her mother would have got nothing...Uncle Albert was the nicest fellow you could imagine – when he was sober." Emily kept the family intact on "next to nowt", as they might say in the milltowns. She hid the money sent to her by her father but Albert usually found it and promptly invested it in liquid assets. Emily had an idea he could smell money!

Helen told me that at their first meeting, daughter Alice had a small sweet shop in Audley Range. She also sold pies, mainly to men from the brickworks. "Annie, her sister, used to help about home and in the shop, and that was how she met her husband. He came across the road from the brickworks in his dinner hour and bought a hot pie."

When Annie had a daughter, Joan, she had a short time off work after the birth; then Joan was cared for by her paternal grandmother, Elizabeth Duxbury, a red-haired Irishwoman. Until starting school, Joan lived during the week in her father's boyhood home, a cottage in Stanhill, and was happy there, partly perhaps because Grandma was not a proud housewife. She did not fuss about minor matters such as having clean clothes or hands.

AW was a bright lad, always top of his class. He had a childhood love of walking and drawing – two accomplishments that would give distinction to his later life. He left school when he was thirteen years old, with little in the way of learning. Most of his contemporaries found menial jobs in the mills. AW was aware that if he wanted to "get on", he had to pass exams. He studied English and literature, which made him a stickler for the correct use of language. He made a special point of correctly using words and criticised the way people spoke.

AW had the brains and good fortune to become an office boy at the Blackburn Borough Engineer's Department. At night school, he studied accountancy. And in his spare time, he continued to demonstrate his flair for art by copying cartoon characters into a notebook. To please his mother, AW attended the aforementioned Furthergate Chapel. (This building was demolished and re-built as Westbury Gardens United Reformed church, not far from the Wainwright home in Audley Range.)

It was at Chapel that he met Ruth Holden, a friend of his sister. Ruth, a weaver, was the only girl he got to know as a young man. Her parents having died, the friendship was based partly on the fact that Ruth's home offered a quiet haven when he was studying for examinations. Home life in Audley Range was constricted and noisy.

When he proposed marriage to Ruth, he was surprised when she accepted him.

"Nobody ever regarded me with admiration. So when one at last showed an interest, I married her." The wedding took place at the Furthergate Congregational chapel, on Christmas Eve, 1931. Bill, Annie's husband, was the best man, and Annie a bridesmaid. The honeymoon cost AW and his new wife a florin – the price of two seats at a local cinema! A son, Peter, was born in 1933.

When AW began serious hill-walking, it was with his son, then aged seven. One trip was to the austere but beautiful limestone hills at the head of Malhamdale. In contrast was the excitement of football. He followed the fortunes of Blackburn Rovers throughout his life. When he lived in the town, and Rovers had a home game, AW was usually among the spectators. He was quietly proud of the history of this Club, which in 1888 was one of the founders of the Football League. It rose to play in the Premier League. When living at Kendal, a Saturday ritual for AW was to switch on the radio for the football results.

AW's job-switch from Blackburn Town Hall to the Borough Treasurer's department at Kendal, at a relatively small salary, brought him nearer to what had become his beloved Lakeland hills. (He was appointed Borough Treasurer in 1948 and held the position until he retired in 1967. Three weeks earlier, his marriage to Ruth came to an end when she walked out; he had treated her unfairly. They were later divorced.)

AW could not forget the trials of his milltown life. He regularly viewed Coronation Street, the television "soap opera", and was to recall something of his native haunts in his book Fellwanderer (1966) – the flickering gas lamps, hot-potato carts, fish and chip shops, public houses and Saturday matinees at the cinema known, not without justification, as "the flea-pit".

He remained "partial" to fish and chips – a quick, hot meal costing just a few coppers. It appealed to married women who worked in the mills and had little time to prepare an evening meal. A virtue of fish-and-chippery was that the ratio of fish to chips need not be constant. In affluent times, a portion of fish per person might be bought. The fish might be divided between three or four, using the cheaper chips to make up the rest of the meal. In some frugal Blackburn households, fish was never made available to the children.

When the aforementioned Helen Lund moved to Bentham in 1946, she heard that AW, his wife and son, were living in a Council house at Kendal. "My mother and I went to see him at his first home in the town. Sometimes we would call at the Town Hall and chat with him in his office. Mother was very fond of him. He reminded her of her sister, AW's mother."

They visited him when he was beginning to produce ink drawings of Lakeland hills. "He gave us one each. I have one of Ashness Bridge. I gave the other to my brother." AW was living on his own. Offered a drink, she received it in a beaker that had been

38 Kendal Green. Kendal
19th May 1985

Dear Doris,

First of all, thankyou for having me last month. It was a welcome change for me, and greatly enjoyed.

The day after my return was the day fixed for the ascent of Penyghent with the BBC team, and fortunately we were favoured with a brilliantly sunny day. I managed to get to the top, very slowly, in spite of a strong and cold east wind and I think everything went off all right. The BBC team, eight of them, are all very young, in their teens and twenties, even the producer being only in his mid thirties. I get on well with all of them and Betty enjoys their company.

Since then I have been kept fully occupied. The managing Director of Michael Josephs has been over to see me with a request that I do more books for them, but it seems unlikely that I will be able to. My eyes are getting worse.

There is also a proposal afoot by the Cumbria Tourist Association to set aside a room in Brantwood (John Ruskin's house at Coniston, open to the public) as a Wainwright Memorial Room with a permanent display of my original manuscripts, drawings and so on. I am lukewarm about the idea, especially their intention to have a bust made of me, but the Gazette are very enthusiastic and I think the scheme will develop.

There is also a great deal of publicity going on by the Gazette to find the purchaser of the millionth book which has just been published secretly but specially marked. When the purchaser has been found he is to be given a free week's holiday in an hotel in the Lake District and I have to present him at a dinner with a set of table mats made from my drawings. These sets are selling at £170!

Last week I was with the BBC team again, this time at Haweswater. On the day arranged for filming the weather was awful, with continuous rain, and nothing could be done, but we went there again on the following day and enjoyed a simply glorious walk with the cameras. I almost enjoyed the experience! Next month we are due in Teesdale.

The Pennine Way book is to be published on June 12th with a fanfare of publicity. The demand is so great that the publishers have had to order a reprint before publication. I have declined an invitation to be a guest of honour at a celebration at Malham in June, when my fellow guests were to be Mike Harding and Barbara Castle. No thanks!

*The football season ended with disappointment for the Rovers, but I have no regrets. They are not good enough for promotion. No need to send any more cuttings, thanks*

*Cousin Eric at Penrissone has been in hospital for ten weeks and is back home but bedfast. I must try to get over to see him later in the summer.*

*I think that's all my news. I was sorry to learn you had suffered another fall and hope it had no serious effects and that you and Cindy are both well.*

*Hope to see you here soon.*

*Love from Betty and myself to you both.*

*AW/alfm*

*The lengthy letter sent by AW to his lifelong friend, Doris Snape, in May 1985.*

filled to the brim. AW asked her if she would like some milk in it. There was, of course, no room for milk. Helen realised that in his solitude AW was not coping very well.

A continuing strong link with Blackburn was his friendship with Doris Snape (nee Garside), of 20 Ramsgreave Drive, the widow of Tom Snape, who had been AW's best friend since they were teenagers. Tom opened a shop in Blackburn at which he sold bicycles. When the cost of repairs was raised, radio sets were offered as part-exchange. Tom, who eventually had many radio sets in his shop, began to hire them out at a weekly rate. It was the start of Radio Rentals.

Alas, Tom died when he was only in his forties. Colin Etherington, a nephew of Doris, informed me that two years later, AW – who had kept in touch with Doris – asked her if she would marry him. She declined, remarking that she did not want to marry anybody. "I loved Tom. I'll always love him. But, if you wish, I'll be your friend for as long as you want." [Doris never married again – and she lived into her nineties.]

Auntie Doris was "well off" [financially sound]. The friendship between AW and Doris lasted for many years. When he married Betty, Doris was invited to the wedding. Colin recalls: "Betty and Alf used to go to my Auntie Doris's for several days at a time. They were all good friends together."

AW, in a long letter to Doris dated 19 May, 1985, thanked her for her hospitality in the previous month. "It was a welcome change for me, and greatly appreciated." He reported on recent and current activities: "The day after my return was the day fixed for the ascent of Penyghent with the BBC team, and fortunately we were favoured with a brilliantly sunny day. I managed to get to the top, very slowly, in spite of a strong and cold east wind and I think everything went off all right. The BBC team, eight of them, are all very young, in their teens and twenties. The producer was only in his mid-thirties. I got on well with all of them and Betty enjoys their company."

Since then, AW had been kept fully occupied. "The Managing Director of Michael Josephs has been over to see me with a request that I do more books for them, but it seems unlikely that I will be able to. My eyes are getting worse."

He mentioned a proposal afoot by the Cumbria Tourist Association to set aside a room in Brantwood, John Ruskin's house at Coniston, which was open to the public, as a Wainwright Memorial Room, "with a permanent display of my original manuscripts, drawings and so on. I am luke-warm about the idea, especially their intention to have a bust made of me, but the Gazette are very enthusiastic and I think the scheme will develop."

AW continued: "There is also a great deal of publicity going on by the Gazette to find the purchaser of the millionth book, which has been published recently but specially marked. When the purchaser has been found he is to be given a full week's holiday in a hotel in the Lake District and I have to present him at a dinner with a set of table mats made from my drawings. These sets are selling at £170!"

In the previous week he had been with the BBC team again, this time at Haweswater. "On the day arranged for filming, the weather was awful, with continuous rain, and nothing could be done, but we went there again on the following day and enjoyed a simply glorious walk with the cameras. I almost enjoyed the experience! Next month we are due in Teesdale."

AW's letter to Doris continued: "The Pennine Way book is to be published on June 12th, with a fanfare of publicity. The demand is so great that the publishers have had to order a reprint before publication. I have declined an invitation to be a guest of honour at a celebration at Malham in June, when my fellow guests were to be Mike Harding and Barbara Castle. No thanks!" [He abhorred crowds.]

AW's next thought was about Blackburn Rovers, his favourite team. "The football season ended with disappointment for the Rovers, but I have no regrets. They are not good enough for promotion. No need to send any more cuttings, thanks." [Doris sent to AW's home in Kendal every cutting of Rovers matches that were published in the Blackburn Times.]

*Bill Duxbury and Annie Wainwright standing, with Ruth Holden (later Wainwright) and AW as witnesses. September 1929.*

*Annie, Bill and
Ruth Wainwright,
early 1950s.*

*Ruth Wainwright
(on left) in 1960.*

*AW's son Peter (left)
with cousins Alan
Fish (centre) and
Jack Fish, 1951.*

He concluded his letter: "I think that's all my news. I was sorry to learn you had suffered another fall and hope it had no serious effects and that you and Cindy are both well. Hope to see you here soon. Love from Betty and myself to you both. Alf xx."

How would Colin sum up Wainwright? "I only knew him when I was a little boy. [AW would have been in his mid-to-late forties.] I might have a different opinion of him if I knew him now. I couldn't speak to him because he did not really want to speak to me."

AW visited Auntie Doris – and then he went to watch Blackburn Rovers play; this team was his passion. "If I ever said anything about Blackburn Rovers, he dismissed me as though he did not want to discuss the matter with me. So I never really got to talk to him very much. I didn't find him easy."

Colin has a postcard which AW wrote to Doris from Newton Stewart, Scotland, posting the card from Wigton in May, 1984. He reported: "A very wet morning after three sunny days. The countryside and coast are beautiful around here, and the cottage we have hired is excellent: very quiet and sheltered by a fine forest with deer. Feeling very fit. Alf xx."

*Chapter Three*

# A Passion for hill-walking – Artist-writer at Work – The Secret Places – A Little Rowan Tree.

As a small boy in Blackburn, AW developed a love for high and lonely places. Whenever possible, he escaped to the hills. His interest in exploring them was fed by a expanding literature and the availability of maps. Some boyhood interests came and went; his love of hill walking not only remained – it developed into a passion.

AW earned his daily bread in the finance department of Kendal Borough Council. Never mercenary, he undertook voluntary work in the town. He laboured conscientiously for six days – and on the seventh he might be seen standing at a Kendal bus stop, awaiting transport into the fell-country. He would chose a fell and, on the spot, analyse its characteristics. This was done with the thoroughness of a doctor giving a patient a medical examination.

He studied its structure, then worked out the best ways to get to the top – a lone explorer on what to him was the next best thing to Himalayan peaks. He was keen to record what clear-weather views were possible from the summit. Soon he was absorbed by the task of recording and keen to do it in a stylish way. Back home, in bursts of energy and artistic flair, he worked on drawings and diagrams.

He foresaw not just a book but a veritable series of guide books. There would be information about 214 fells in all. The first to be published dealt with the Eastern Fells, its style and standard being maintained, unwaveringly, in the years to come. This enormous feat of penmanship had begun at his home on the evening of November 9, 1952. Living alone, his cat excepted, he portrayed on a single page a popular route up Dove Crag. He gave his imagination free play, being "lost to all else...I was working for my own pleasure and enjoying it hugely."

His re-creation of Lakeland fells on paper was a task done slowly, meticulously, with the utmost care, using a fine-nibbed pen. He welcomed the introduction of maps that were two-and-a-half inches to the mile and to photographs taken with a second-hand camera, one of the bellows type. It had "various contrivances" but AW limited himself to the knob he must press to take a picture. He shrewdly took into account the fact

*Grasmere, ringed by misty fells.*

that a camera lens tends to depress verticals and extend distances. At the rate of one page an evening, he drew the fells precisely as they are and not as an artist might image them.

Graduating to maps of six-inch scale, he now had the patterns created by roads, paths and drystone walls. He was able to record old sheepfolds and also in his mind were "the wild gullies and ravines that rarely see a two-legged visitor". Lakeland, noted for its fine scenery, had nonetheless been heavily industrialised. AW now found "the secret places" – adits, levels and shafts of mines and abandoned buildings connected with quarrying. Silence, he wrote, is always more profound in places where once there was noise.

The meticulous task continued but when, in July of 1953, he had prepared a hundred pages of pictures and prose, he scrapped them, finding the raggedness of the line ends unacceptable. They were not "justified", to use a printing term. He did the work again, fitting the lines as neatly as he could to give the illusion of a straight edge. "I never quite succeeded, but the pages looked better than before. They were neater and tidier." He dedicated the first of his guide books to his heroes – the Men of the Ordnance Survey.

His initial venture – six Pictorial Guides (eventually seven) – were brought to breath-taking conclusion over a spell of thirteen years. Outdoors, his fell-walking had been "a dreamlike procession of happy, uneventful days." He never had an accident or a fall. Nor was he ever be-nighted in a blizzard or tossed by a bull! "I always walked alone." He had the consolation, in those early days, of realising that few people would recognise him.

AW occasionally sent me items for publication in Cumbria. One of these tit-bits concerned a little rowan tree – and what happened to it. One day in 1960, he was toiling up the steep trackless gully of Hassnesshow Beck from Buttermere, pioneering a route to the summit of Robinson, when he noticed what appeared to be two twigs sticking upright from a low crag at the side of the ravine.

Curious, he climbed up to inspect, and found to his surprise that the twigs were in fact the branches of a tiny rowan that had secured a root-hold in a thin crack in the rock face, the seed having evidently blown there or been dropped by a passing bird. With no visible means of sustenance and no root run, it had nevertheless secured a firm hold.

AW observed that rowans are tenacious little beggars in infancy, "yet I had to admire the courage and determination of the puny specimen surviving against all the odds. It seemed to have a message for me. Don't quit. Don't give up. Keep trying." He couldn't forget it. "The lesson it had for me helped me on the rest of the climb. When later I described the route in the book I was writing I mentioned it."

A year or two went by and AW began to receive letters, all assuring him that the rowan was still alive and flourishing. "Since then I have had a great many reports about the state of the tree, and even a poem, from readers all over the country. From their accompanying photographs I have watched it grow in stature over the past 20 years. The year 1970, ten years on, brought a sheaf of correspondence. A party from Whitehaven wrote a saga of their visit, illustrated by camera studies and graphic drawings."

Many years passed, never without several assurances that all was well. AW was mightily pleased to learn that the rowan was now bearing berries and developing quickly. On New Year's Day, 1980, the Whitehaven party made another pilgrimage, braving the snow and ice, to confirm its continuing survival, and again supplied photographs and more dramatic pen-and-ink illustrations of their arduous ascent.

AW commented: "No single feature I have mentioned in my books has brought me more letters, not even Jack's Rake, and they have given me great pleasure. The rowan isn't my tree, but I have developed a proprietary interest in it and think of it as mine. It will outlive me and carry my name as a sort of monument. I could not wish for a better. Some day I will struggle up there again and renew an acquaintance that, with its message, has never been far from my mind since I noticed it in 1960."

In 1966, AW sent me an account of what he dubbed Lakeland's oddest treasure hunt. He doubted whether anyone would trouble to read the chapter he wrote describing Lank Rigg. On a sunny afternoon in April, 1965, he placed a 1950 florin underneath a flat stone near the Ordnance Survey column on the summit. "I thought it would stay there for ever unless I retrieved it myself because Lank Rigg is an unknown and unloved fell and its summit, far removed from places of popular tourist resort, is rarely visited by walkers."

He had reckoned without the venturous spirit, or desperate poverty, or rapacious greed, of some of his readers. The hidden treasure was found the day after The Western Fells was published on March 12, at 9-20 a.m. The discoverers were Susan Tosswill of Seaton, Workington, accompanied by her husband Richard and an infant Tosswill. They had made a dawn start and sent AW an entertaining account of the discovery.

A visitor from Asby, Appleby, on that same day, searched unsuccessfully for the Wainwright Florin. He left a paper, inviting fellwalkers to enter their name. When the paper was full, the last finder was requested to send the list to Mr W, c/o the Publishers. A Roll of Honour resulted and on March 22, two visitors from Livepool signed their names on the last bit of space and sent the paper to AW with two colour slides, titled

*Charles Relph, in the yard of Ashness Farm,*
*above Borrowdale.*

*County Stone, the former meeting place of Westmorland, Lancashire and the West Riding of Yorkshire.*

Anticipation and Despair.

On April 5, a Northampton visitor (staying at Glenridding) climbed the fell with his son in a gale. He had the happy thought of leaving a second florin with AW's, if he was not too late. He decided to leave a note suggesting that all who came after should do the same, making the summit a collecting station for the RSPCA.

Alas, he found he had been forestalled; the wind snatched his note away from his hand and carried it away towards the Irish Sea. He contented himself by leaving a threepenny piece on the top of the column to console the next comer and reported that the top of the fell looked as though a bulldozer had been over it, every stone within sight having been overturned.

AW congratulated Susan, the early bird, and commiserated with the others. "It is Lank Rigg I really feel sorry for. Lank Rigg is feminine, and very prim and proper; in fact something of a prude, brought up to a life of seclusion. She must be feeling highly indignant that her quiet summit has been violated thus." He continued: "The Ancient Britons who built the nearby tumulus and the Ordnance people who erected the triangulation column were perfect gentlemen, but, really, those awful disrespectful, plundering fortune-hunters of recent weeks…"

AW added: "Let's leave Lank Rigg alone now to recover from her wounds and regain her former tranquillity and composure. I ought to have known better. Thank goodness it wasn't half-a-crown!"

*Chapter Four*

# A Silent Interview with AW – Westmorland Heritage – To Hadrian's Wall – Limestone Country.

Harry Firth, a brisk, efficient and kindly Bradfordian, presided over the staff at the Gazette works in Kendal where AW's novel pictorial guide was printed. A staff accustomed to deal with hard type and metal blocks – almost a blacksmith's job – found AW's hand-drawn and written art work an appealing novelty.

My first glimpse of AW's handiwork occurred on an otherwise dull day in 1954. Harry Firth, arriving at our office unexpectedly, slowly unwrapped a parcel to reveal the pages of AW's first guide, dealing with the Eastern Fells. This was to be the first of many instalments of his "love letters for Lakeland." I had the spine-tingling sensation that Howard Carter must have experienced when he first glimpsed the contents of Tutankhamen's tomb. Like Carter, I saw wonderful things!

After much thought, AW had taken his Book One – his "little infant" – to Sandy Hewitson, a local printer, who assessed costs and proclaimed that 2,000 copies was an economical must. The cost? Sandy was not out to "fleece" a fellow Kendalian but the price, a swingeing £950, was £915 more than the author/artist possessed. Trustingly, it was arranged that he would pay for the work from the income derived from books that were sold.

Henry Bateman, the Kendal Librarian, undertook the distribution and despatch of books, his name appeared as publisher on the title page of the first volume. This arrangement soon collapsed through weight of numbers, which left business matters to AW. He was relieved when, in 1963, the Gazette offered to take over their publication.

On successive visits to the Gazette printing department to attend to issues of our magazine Cumbria, I experienced the Wainwrightian revolution, passing between white cliffs of paper allocated for his work. After the first satisfactory demand, sales fell away. AW paid for a full-page advert in Cumbria and I was allowed to print a specimen page in each of our monthly magazines, bringing the project to the attention of a world-wide circulation of around 90,000.

*AW and colleagues in the finance department at the Town Hall, Kendal. (A photograph displayed at a commemorative exhibition in the town).*

Harry Firth also arranged for me to interview AW. At this stage, he was agreeable to anything that would publicise his book. The meeting with Mr Wainwright – those were respectful days – took place in the Borough Treasurer's department of Kendal Town Hall. A side door and a flight of steps brought me into the large, old-fashioned, somewhat dowdy office AW had occupied since 1948. I was offered a chair. We sat in Quakerish silence.

AW was a dapper man in clothes of subdued hues. Yet here was a man who considered that "fellwalking is action and fellwalking is fun." With tweedy clothes, he seemed to merge with his desk, fidgetted with a smoking pipe and spoke infrequently. I had been hoping he would tell me of his week-end wanderings in what he had called "silent and lonely places." In the slow passage of yawn-repressing time, I had a feeling of being at the birth of a new style of journalism. The wordless interview.

AW shyly produced a drawing from the top drawer of his desk. With the drawer open, I glimpsed some of his art material – a simple pen, the type used in schools, and a bottle of Indian ink. The sketch he produced was a partly completed study of a Lakeland fell. There was enough to convey by its outline and distinctive character a feeling that AW, as an artist, had the ability to give hills a sense of life.

He thawed a little. How many words did I propose to write about him? More technical questions. What style would I adopt? How long would it take me to do it? It was, of course, a brush-off. I negotiated a postal interview. I would send him several questions. He would return them, with answers, in my stamped addressed envelope. At least, I would have something to show for my afternoon's work.

AW dutifully filled in the answers to my questions, presumably re-used my stamped envelope, then put the questionaire aside at his home on Kendal Green. It pleased me to know that a little bit of me had found its way into his files. Years would pass before the material surfaced and I might read the answers to the questions I had posed – by post.

My old friend Hunter Davies, researching among family papers for a biography of AW, found a sheet with typed (and corrected) answers to my questions. He presented them in an article published in Cumbria; they appeared in their entirety in his biography. My first question had been: what had impelled AW to write the book? He had an idea. "Ideas grow, like habits, until they become a way of life." It might even have dated to his boyhood, when he already had a passion for hill-walking. Other enthusiasts came and went "but my love of the fells has been constant."

He gloried in mountain country. He was inspired by mountain literature. His favourite reading was a map. AW even had a boyhood ambition to climb Everest, even to die on its summit! With increasing age, his ambitions were modified. The fells took the place of Everest, providing an outlet for the climbing and exploring urge fostered by

This is to announce the publication of a book
that is quite out of the ordinary

• Primarily it is a book for fellwalkers, for those who know
the fells intimately and for those who know them but little •
It is a book for all lovers of Lakeland
It is a book for collectors of unusual books

It is the first volume of a series under the title of
**A PICTORIAL GUIDE TO THE LAKELAND FELLS**

This first volume is
BOOK ONE : THE EASTERN FELLS
describing the Helvellyn and Fairfield groups

Hand-printed throughout, with 500 illustrations
(drawings, maps and diagrams) in its 300 pages,
it represents an original idea in the making of books
• The author is *Alfred Wainwright* of Kendal

Its price is twelve shillings and sixpence
Copies are obtainable from bookshops in Lakeland,
or by post (for sixpence more) from HENRY MARSHALL,
LOW BRIDGE, KENTMERE, WESTMORLAND

*The first advertisement for a Wainwright book, Cumbria magazine, June 1955.*

*AW, photographed  in 1988.*

the many books of mountain travel. If only I had known that the man at whose desk I sat had such thoughts racing through his mind at the time of our meeting.

He had planned his walks as though conducting a military campaign. "You remember the war maps, the black arrows of advancing troops, the pincer movements, the mopping-up operations. That's the way I worked, but my thoughts were not of war, but utterly of peace." Why was the first of the books hand-written and hand-drawn? "Because the book was intended originally only as a personal chronicle of my observations, so that everything in it, the notes as well as the illustrations, was prepared by hand."

My next written question had been: have you had any training in art or book illustration? He hadn't but, for years, much of his leisuretime was spent translating into pictures his vivid impressions of the Lakeland fells. While building up a favourite mountain from a blank sheet of paper, he might experience the subtle joy of feeling he was physically engaged on the ascent as the familiar shape came into being under the pen.

To AW this was a discovery of some importance. "I could now sit in my chair on a winter's evening and bring Scafell or Gable into the room with me. When I could not go to the hills I could make them come to me." Did he always go alone? Invariably. He preferred to go alone. He must be alone if he was to get any work done.

Not being technically minded, and retiring in 1967, AW avoided the computing age of accountancy. In his career, ledgers and cash books were hand-written, in AW's case – immaculately. Percy Duff, a colleague, admired AW's determination and single-mindedness when working on his guide books. As soon as one was finished, he would start on the next. This pen-and-ink man – to use one of his phrases – could not sit back.

In his young days, AW was shy, skinny and ungainly. He was fond of walking and realised an early ambition at the age of 23 when, having a break from work and some cash to spare, he and a cousin travelled the sixty miles to Lakeland for a walking holiday. The year was 1930. In seven days his life was changed. As mentioned, he ascended Orrest Head, a hill of moderate height. Looking westwards, he was "utterly enslaved by all I saw...here were no huge factories, but mountains; no stagnant canals, but sparkling, crystal-clear rivers, no cinder paths but beckoning tracks that climbed through bracken and heather to the silent fastnesses of the hills."

My first Wainwright purchase, in 1966, was a hardback, landscape style, published by the Gazette and giving the well-illustrated story behind the pictorial guides to the Lakeland Fells he compiled, primarily for his own pleasure, between 1952 and 1965. I was charmed by his art work and the prose that enwrapped it. For example, AW asserted that all the best tracks had been made by sheep. The routes they had habitually

*A gathering of Herdwick sheep.*

taken were "the oldest highways on the hills and the best."

The least-known, and among the most prized, of my Wainwright books is Westmorland Heritage, the weighty tome, landscape format, hand-written and liberally illustrated throughout. Devising it was prompted by a governmental reorganisation of the county boundaries that came into effect on the last day of March, 1974. It destroyed, except in retrospect, the old county pride. Westmorland lost its identity, being absorbed in the newly-created county of Cumbria.

This AW tribute to Westmorland was printed and published as a limited edition (one thousand copies) by the Gazette at Kendal in 1975. The dedication was "to those who have their roots in Westmorland." He confessed that, an offcomer, he was introduced to Westmorland only in middle life. My copy of the book is numbered 242 and signed by the author in his favoured green ink. AW made it known that he did not want a second edition of the book to be considered.

Like AW, I had a considerable nostalgia for t'old days. In the book he had described and pictured Westmorland as it was – "a distinctive region of fields and farms, fells and mountains, everywhere pleasant, free from heavy industry, independent and having little in common with neighbouring areas into whose company they were thrust." The Westmerians liked the name of their county. "They liked to be able to call Westmorland their very own."

Parishes were dealt with in alphabetical order. He described the little-known Fawcett Forest as "a parish with few habitations, few people and thousands of sheep. Mainly rough moorland, it rises to around 1,800-ft between the valleys of Bannisdale and Borrowdale." Here were "rolling fells but no exciting mountains." Yet "the landscape, with a quieter beauty, is more typically Westmorland than the frequented Langdales and Grasmere." AW's writing style proved to be as engaging as the art work.

Another favourite book dates from the autumn of 1938. As war clouds were gathering, AW walked along the Pennine spine from Settle to Hadrian's Wall and back again on a different route. His record of the excursion, A Pennine Journey, was published unaltered half a century after it was written. It is a literary classic. Ill-clothed, his footwear was a single pair of low shoes that suffered badly from harsh weather and boggy or rocky terrain. He deflected the heaviest rain via a folded cape.

Nothing cheers me up more than reading of his Pennine walk and of his (often amusing) encounters with local folk. Wainwright was a man with a profound, even spiritual, love of the hills (Good Housekeeping) writing a book that was gentle, wise and idyllic (Sunday Express). In the late 1930s, the notion of nations fighting each other seemed incongruous when considered by a solitary walker on desolate Pennine moors, where his companions were larks, curlews and sheep. He did not meet another walker in the fortnight he was out and about on the heights.

AW, having the Pennines to himself, found that they provided the comfort and reassurance he badly needed. He fantasised a good deal. The Pennines run north and south. Separate hills forming the range were the vertebrae. Ridges of high moors stretching eastwards were ribs and between the ribs lay the arteries, the rivers. "A queer skeleton this, with ribs on one side only, for there are none on the west. But its flesh is firm and solid, and purple with heather."

On the last night, in Dentdale, he went through a fanciful mental love-making process - with a hot water bottle. When AW was back in Settle, walking along busy streets to the railway station, he felt conspicuous – unkempt, with dirty clothes and shoes on the point of collapse. The heels had gone and the soles were fast-falling to pieces, which forced him to slur his feet as he walked.

Sixty-one years later, four of us – Bob, Stan, Colin and myself, disciples of Wainwright – visited the Wall, inspired by his prose and clad in state-of-the art rambling wear. It was our intention to walk along it, rather than to and from it. We would begin perversely at Wallsend and our expedition would end at Bowness by the Solway.

We saved time by travelling to the Borders by car and indeed split the walk into manageable sections and arranged to have a car at each end. At Throckley we caught a Metro train to Wallsend. A native asked: "Weer's the Gannin'?" We had about ten miles of pavement-pounding, which AW would have hated. Near Segedunum, we passed what looked like a building site but was in reality the restoration of a Roman fort of that name. We strode through housing estates where the streets were named after ancient Roman dignitaries.

Stan several times came to an abrupt halt as the spike of his tubular metal stick lodged in urban cracks. (AW did not have need for a stick). We buttied near the cathedral, getting a disdainful look from a passing cleric. We visited the Byker City Farm, in the (still verdant) Ouseburn Valley, meeting a Rhode Island Red cockerel that, according to an attendant, might be enticed to jump six feet for a biscuit. No one had a biscuit.

On the old Roman route out of town, we had the recurrent tang of fish and chips, which would have appealed to AW, who was a chish and fip addict. Jackie's pub advertised: "Win or lose – we'll have some booze." Up, up, up we strode on Westgate Hill, passing dozens of motor bike shops. In Roman times the goods on view would doubtless be chariots of various sizes.

Bits of preserved Wall came into view. The best section – and it was not extensive – lay exposed, replastered, maybe even sanitised, near Charlie Brown's garage. An ultra-modern touch was provided when Concorde, the most modern aircraft, a white dart, nose up, undercarriage down, was seen in a gradual descent towards Newcastle Airport.

The Tyne Valley was patchy with fields of yellow rape. At Haddon, where another stretch of wall was exposed, Stan wondered why the Wall as so thick. Bob said it was because people had to walk on it. Colin: "If it was any thinner, they'd tend to fall off." At Rudcaster Farm, we left the line of the wall (now a major and busy road) for quieter places. Skylarks rose like feathered helicopters. A corn bunting uttered its scratchy refrain and a yellow hammer mused incessantly about "a little bit of bread and no c-h-e-e-s-e."

We used paths across arable land. A jungle of rape speckled our trousers with yellow. We negotiated a field of waist-high corn, following what should have a path and with no handy alternative route. After the arable episode, walking conditions between Chollerford and Corbridge could not have been more attractive. Following a riverside path, we saw a sparkle on the Tyne and detected a coconutty tang emanating from flowering gorse. There was a hatch of orange-tip butterflies.

On to Hexham, where we were treated to the unexpected sight of – three elephants, among the cast at Robert's Circus. Small children were feeding them with grass. Across the river, we regained the hills, thence to Acomb, where we stopped outside (then inside) the Miner's Arms, conspicuously dated 1750. On the top shelf, behind the bar, was a model of a miner, complete with lamp.

Our first real insight into Roman life came at Chesters. Here were the substantial remains of a fort at which a cavalry unit was stationed. Inside the museum was a model of the place as it might have been and a river bridge that no longer exists. There were gods galore – both Roman and Celtic gods. Presumably after worshipping the Emperor, the Romans might take their pick of the deities they wished to adore.

We entered the Northumbria National Park, its emblem a curlew in flight. When we had quit the valley for the breezy heights, curlews were calling all around us. I fancy that the bubbling song of the curlew cheered AW on his lonesome walks. We did a bit of trespassing to see another stretch of wall. Colin referred to our "Right to Rome".

Leaving a tediously long stretch of road, we made a diagonal approach to Sewingshields, the range of crags across the top of which the Romans set their Wall. This was undoubtedly the highlight of our expedition. Glancing over a well-preserved stump of Wall, we viewed the big country extending northwards into Scotland, the horizon tinged by the dark green of the mainly coniferous Border Forest.

*Top: East of Housesteads Fort, on the Roman Wall.*

*Bottom: A section of the Roman Wall.*

*Wainwright pipe and drawings as displayed in an exhibition at Abbot Hall, Kendal.*

Black-faced sheep, with strong lambs at foot, romped about the crags with the verve of goats. (AW acknowledged the worth of sheep as unofficial green-keepers). Two ponies performed a ballet of graceful movement in close company. Then, tiring of the sport, settled down to more grazing. Housesteads was under attack from school parties. We sneaked in, admired the design of the latrine block in the south-east corner of the fort and, ere long, sneaked out again. As, indeed, AW would have done.

He, like us, would have been anxious to bestride the Wall in its most picturesque stretch, on an undulating ridge, overlooking the swan-ruffled water of Crag Lough. Westwards lay the Nine Nicks of Thirwall, where the escarpment had the undulations of a Big Dipper, and an area where a television company had been laying out props for filming a story of a man who lives rough on the hills. The filmsters had modern conveniences, including a "Borderloo", resembling Dr Who's telephone box and with a similar blue colouration.

Eventually, we were in an area where the Wall was superseded by what had originally been a barrier made of turf. (This would have had little appeal for AW, who hankered after high ground).We entered the Carlisle area at Harraby, a place of grand houses and a stud, which was appropriate, for at nearby Stanwix the Romans had a huge

*AW with his favourite reading – an Ordnance Survey map.*

*Limestone country above the market town of Settle, North Ribblesdale.*

cavalry base. From Carlisle, the hills were left behind; the last few miles of our walk along the Wall were on a road that seemed to have been laid using a spirit level, with marshland on either side and the Solway gleaming to the north.

Outside the terminating feature – a pub at Bowness-on-Solway – we had five minutes to wait before opening time. We were treated to entertaining tales from post-Roman times. One day, the pub was opened up at 6 p.m to admit a score of hungry men dressed as Jacobites. An entry in the visitors' book concerned a man whose only memory of the start of a great adventure was a flashing blue light as an ambulance conveyed him to Carlisle Infirmary. He had slipped a few yards into the walk, fracturing a leg.

The AW who first took to the fells was lean and lish. (Later photographs and BBC films about his excursions in Lakeland, the Pennines and Scotland, revealed a somewhat puffy figure.) His beloved smoking pipe was in his mouth. Wisps of grey hair trailed over the collar of his coat. He walked haltingly, frequently stopping to admire the scene.

When Sue Lawley, of the BBC, suggested in Desert Island Discs that his guide book work might interfere with the claims of his marriage, he insensitively remarked that

*Top left: Limestone pavement on Giggleswick Scar.*

*Top right: Ingleborough, as seen from Chapel-le-Dale.*

one evening Ruth and the dog had gone for a walk – and he'd never seen them again. (The rest of the extended Wainwright family loved his good-natured wife.) Outdoors, he avoided other walkers by moving rapidly under cover. He said he did not like being on the stage; his place was out of sight in the wings!

AW refused to be photographed. If he included a sketch of himself in a book, the figure, pipe in mouth, would be kept small, facing away. In my files at the magazine Cumbria I had a snap of him in profile, complete with pipe, a distinctive shock of hair protruding from under his cap. Not wishing to upset him, when I took the picture out of its file, at least once a year, I would sigh - and return it to its inconspicuous retreat. In the end, I lost track of it...

AW compiled a notable guide book to the Pennine Way, a matter of 250 miles from

*Looking eastwards from the summit plateau of Ingleborough.*

*Whernside, highest point in the Yorkshire Dales National Park, as viewed from Ingleborough.*

Edale in Derbyshire to Kirk Yetholm in Scotland. The writer Ivor Brown had called this protracted footway "the Great North Roof." Walk along the Pennine Way and you pass through a succession of solitudes. Everywhere there are sheep. The other sounds, in spring, emanate from upland wading birds, here for the breeding season. Curlew, golden plover, lapwing and snipe form a fluty ensemble. The tawny landscape unfolds slowly, rather like the plot of a good book. Interest is sustained to the end.

AW was aware that the Pennine Way was first suggested in 1935 by Tom Stephenson, who mentioned it as an idea in a newspaper article. Possible routes were surveyed before the 1939-45 war. The National Parks Commission made the Way the first of the long-distance paths. Its recommendation was approved in 1951 but many years elapsed before the entire route was negotiated with landowners keen to protect their grouse moors from invading pedestrians.

The Pennine Way was officially opened in the springtime of 1965 and I was among the 2,000 people who gathered near Malham Tarn for the ceremony. Tents sprouted like giant mushrooms on tussocky ground that was still drained of its colour. Spring was a little late that year.

I wondered how many people in the vast crowed were aware that the name Pennines began as a hoax. It seems that Charles Bertram, who was teaching English in a naval college at Copenhagen, assembled details of Britain in Roman times and cooked up the mixture in Latin to describe Roman Britain. The author purported it had been written by a monk of Westminster Abbey. Among the spurious names was Alpes Penina, for our northern hill range. Today, any other name for the Pennine uplift would be unthinkable.

AW's Pennine Way Companion was published by the Westmorland Gazette in 1968. The form and style were familiar to those who knew the earlier books: the detailed maps that showed every pool and wall and cairn; the neat and useful little sketches; the hand-printed description of every mile of the Way. Yet originality, as well as humour, crept into this book as in the earlier guides.

Surprisingly, the book began at the end of the walk and finished with the start, for the practical reason that most people do the walk from south to north up the map. So by beginning at the last page, you walk up to that to the next and begin at the bottom again. "Ultimately," wrote AW, "if you don't give up or get lost, you will arrive at Kirk Yetholm at the top of page 5".

He greeted each successful walker with the "You will be a better man because you have walked the Pennine Way. Well done!" He left money at the pub in Kirk Yetholm to provide a pint of beer to each successful walker. (It was later reduced to half a pint. So popular was the walk, the reward had to be abolished in the interests of solvency.)

AW was fond of walking in the Craven district, where limestone lights up the landscape. In his book Walks in Limestone Country, we had a pocket size version of a larger production. In the process, a good deal of the hand-written directions had to be reduced in size to the point at which reading is not easy. Some people might have to carry a magnifying glass as well as the book. Even then, it would be worth the effort.

There were the expected piquant comments. At The Dalesman, it gave us pride to note what he wrote about an ascent of Ingleborough from this village. "Of the many walks described in this book, the ascent of Ingleborough from Clapham is pre-eminent, the finest of all, a classic. A lovely village...charming woodlands...an enchanting valley...natural wonders...and a climb to a grand mountain top. Oh, yes, this is the best."

Ingleborough, one of the big Pennine flat-tops, almost shouts to be noticed. A local farmer described it as "a big rough hill. And wild! The wind is sometimes strong enough to blow a sheep over. I wouldn't be capped [surprised] to see snow up there on Midsummer's Day." AW was aware that when the steep north face was in shadow this was a Big Blue Hill. Laurence Binyon, the young son of the Vicar of Burton-in-Lonsdale, whose bedroom window framed a view of Ingleborough, grew up to be an academic and poet, author of Words to the Fallen.

The Young Binyon had been inspired by Ingleborough to write his first poem:

> *To a bare blue hill*
> *Wings an old thought roaming,*
> *At a random touch*
> *Of memory homing.*
>
> *The first of England*
> *These eyes to fill*
> *Was the lifted head*
> *Of that proud hill...*

AW noted that Ingleborough has the advantage, shared by only a few mountains, of a shapely outline from whatever direction it is seen. Rising in glorious isolation from valleys on all sides, this celebrated hill gave the impression of being higher than it is.

*Chapter Five*

# A Chat with Harry Griffin – The Bad Step – On Fleetwith Pike – Television Debut.

In his book Freedom of the Hills published in 1978, Harry Griffin mentioned his long-time friendship with AW and confessed that he had never taken one of his guides onto the hills. "In my view, these guide books are for study at home – preferably after you have explored a particular area – and not as replacements for map and compass."

More than once, he and AW argued this point of view, agreeing only to differ. I arrived at Harry's house determined to broach the topic of Wainwright guides while simply following the old Cumbrian habit of "dropping in" for a crack [chat] and a cup of tea. Harry, warmly clad as though for a walk on Helvellyn, was about to apply himself to gardening on a day when there was a sneaky easterly wind.

I had read in Harry's latest book that in his 67th year he set himself what he considered to be the very modest challenge: to revisit all the summits of the Lake District in excess of 2,000-ft in height. He set a time limit of three months. Was the project completed within this period? Of course. "With very little extra effort the round could have been completed within two months." Harry afterwards wished he had made that effort!

The Griffins, Harry and Molly, used to live at a stone-built house on Windermere Road [the main road from Kendal to Keswick]. From the window of the lounge, and beyond a lawn that sloped down to the road, a bus stop was situated. Said Harry: "I'd often see Alf standing outside my gate on a Saturday or Sunday morning waiting for the Keswick bus." In A Bit of Grit on Haystacks, a celebration of Wainwright published by Millrace, Harry concluded that AW must have travelled on the Keswick bus scores of times. Not having a car, it was the handiest way of reaching the base of his chosen fells.

Re-reading AW's guides, Harry had sensed a current of sadness running through the series. Each area would be loved for perhaps two years. It was then perhaps never to be revisited. He said as much on the completion of his fourth book, on The Southern Fells. Harry confessed: "This same feeling has always haunted the fells for me."

The Griffins moved to a bungalow they had built at the end of Cunswick Scar, near Kendal. "It suited our needs." The windows framed some of the fairest views in Cumbria. Of course, they had to pay for their fine position hundreds of feet above sea level, with nothing between them – weatherwise – and the Shap Fells. The biting easterlies came from that direction. During the previous winter, scouring winds destroyed plants that had been in the rockery for twenty years.

To wander around Harry's home was to have a feeling of a house turned inside out. Pictures and artefacts related to the great outdoors. Harry was not simply a fellwanderer, like AW. At the time I met him – and he was by no means young – he averaged a hundred fell-going expeditions a year. His interests were varied. He would go fell-walking, rock-climbing ("but not very much now"), winter-climbing with axes and crampons, also ski-mountaineering.

Said Harry: "I was snow-climbing about ten days ago in a gully on Fairfield. It involved about a thousand feet of step-kicking. The snow was very soft and two, sometimes three, hard kicks were needed to make a single step. At the end of the day I was seized with enormous pains in my thighs..." He spoke, matter-of-factly. A thousand feet of step-cutting was not considered exceptional to him. AW would have thought twice about undertaking it.

He had some forthright views about Wainwright, while counting himself among AW's few real friends. Harry's assessment of AW was – awkward, shy and unsociable but friendly, genuine, straightforward and generous. He had reservations about AW's guides to Lakeland fells, considering that to follow AW's guide to a fells blindly, almost yard by yard, as many people appeared to do, seemed to him to destroy some of the sense of adventure. Admittedly, AW was writing for those who did not know the fells intimately. If the guides had been compiled for more experienced walkers, he would probably have agreed with Harry's point of view.

Had Harry ever taken a Wainwright guide to the fells? He pondered for a moment, then confessed that he did – once. He was on Coomb Height, which at the time was unknown to him. Harry carried the guide book for interest rather than for direction. Inevitably, the guides had a few errors. Harry mentioned to AW an eminence with a cairn which had been stated to be cairnless. AW promptly explained that his guide book had been written fifteen years before, since when new cairns had been "springing up all over the place."

Quite apart from a long association with journalism, Harry had written ten hardback books about the Lake District. His Lakeland articles appeared weekly in the Lancashire Evening Post for forty years. Notes signed AHG adorned The Guardian fortnightly for nearly thirty-six years. When Harry retired, a dozen years before, he wrote a book based on return visits to the fells in the Lake District which are over 2,000-ft and are therefore counted as mountains. There are, he told me, 203 such peaks.

*Borrowdale, viewed from Castle Crag.*

*Time to rest after a steady climb from Borrowdale.*

*Visiting walkers above the Troutbeck Valley.*

Readers of the aforementioned Millrace book of essays about Wainwright will recall Harry Griffin's recollection of being asked by him to be taken to Dove's Nest caves on Rosthwaite Fell near Glaramara. Harry had a torch and some candles. The caves were reached from Borrowdale by way of Comb Gill. The entrance, where lights are needed, is about 20-ft or so up the crag, which was classified as an easy scramble, though to Harry it was hardly a scramble at all.

When AW beheld the "simple scramble", he told Harry, emphatically, that he was not going up there! "However, knowing his antipathy to rock, I had anticipated this, producing a rope I had secreted in my rucksack." AW recoiled from this as if it had been a poisonous snake. "So, he never saw the caves and they are not described, in detail, in his guide."

In a note on the Southern Fells, Harry mentioned Wainwright's "bad step", encountered on the Crinkles, a line of turreted summits providing a fine ridge walk, especially in winter. The "bad step" was on the way up to the second Crinkle from the south. When Harry had gone this way, half a century before, he and his friends had taken the "bad step" easily in their stride. AW, expert in finding these places, even located one on Low Pike above Ambleside. In one of his guides, half a page had been devoted to the Crinkle Crags "bad step". Harry commented: "Perhaps if it hadn't been labelled, it wouldn't seem quite so awesome to the timid."

Wainwright was not a musical type. He liked natural sounds. It had never occurred to me that Harry Griffin was a pianist, but a piano stood in the drawing room; he sat down and played a few bars of Beethoven. "I've been playing the piano for 69 years. "I play every evening for an hour or more." He did not claim to play well, but his knowledge of music was extensive.

Having heard from Harry of his fell-going activities, and not wishing to do anything as extreme as snow-climbing, in 1993 I joined a walker who was setting out to stand on what to him was a mopping up operation – his last few Wainwright fells. There was some snow on the tops. We limbered up on three little peaks flanking Borrowdale on a day when autumn and winter overlapped. It was theoretically autumn, season of mists and mellow fruitfulness. The oaks had tinted leaves, yet the clouds looked wintry and on high ground the "snow dogs" were howling.

A family who had just completed a walk round Derwentwater originally intended to climb Helvellyn. The expedition was aborted when they encountered a foot of snow – on the approach road. We climbed Catbells, with a pair of croaking ravens for company and our feet crunching an inch of compacted hailstones. The ravens were show-offs, occasionally flipping on to their backs to cruise upside down.

Catbells became a vantage point for the autumnal splendour of the Borrowdale oakwoods. Looking in the opposite direction, we saw a majestic assembly of glacier-sculpted fells, dusted white and giving the impression that the Pleistocene Age ended a couple of weeks ago. We trudged up Castle Crag, the smallest of the Wainwrights, with the clink of slate underfoot.

The first of our snack meals was consumed as we enjoyed one of the grandest views in England – through the Jaws of Borrowdale to Derwentwater and Old Man Skiddaw, now robbed of his majesty, swaddled by cloud as thick as cotton wool. We switched our walking to the base of Fleetwith Pike, the fell that gives Buttermere a shapely headpiece.

Since my last visit, a zig-zag path had been created up the lower slope to stop further erosion, which was not only unsightly but dangerous. The whitened cross was still there, reminding us of an accident befalling a Victorian girl who tripped over her Lakeland equivalent of an alpenstock and died in the fall.

In the early stages of the climb, when we had increasingly impressive views of Honister Pass, between its sullen rocks, the weather prospects seemed good. Rays of sunshine, like spotlights in an opera house, played around the scene, picking out one glorious feature after another. The cloud thickened and disgorged hailstones; higher up, flurries of snow added their bulk to the several inches already on the ground.

I allowed my friend to pick the moment to reach the summit. He did so with a fine sense of timing – in a momentary flash of sunlight, which illuminated his blue waterproofs and his arms upheld in a victory sign. He had a six-inch smile. He had passed out as a Wainwrighter. We celebrated his achievement by visiting Buttermere Church to see the window-ledge plaque commemorating Alfred Wainwright. My friend was already contemplating another test set by AW – climbing the summits mentioned in his book on Outlying Fells!

AW was given the high accolade of a television series. This acutely shy man took a good deal of persuasion to appear on t'telly. The BBC producer was Richard Else, who had for long been enthralled by AW's guides ad sketchbooks. He had not attempted to rush AW into a decision about appearing on film. Indeed, writing in the Westmorland Gazette, being one of several close friends assessing the worth of AW on his death, he originally suggested that he did not appear and, instead, there might be a programme in which some of his friends might chat about him.

The BBC filmed the reluctant hero and the first series of programmes was screened in the North East during the autumn of 1985. I recall an evening when I switched on the television to see the 78-year-old AW making his screen debut with broadcaster Eric Robson. They were slowly descending a track on Penyghent. Wainwright films had a national showing, propelling the fellwalker – difficult, taciturn, cumbersome though he might be in his old age – into stardom. Eventually, the BBC film tours took in Yorkshire, Lakeland and Scotland.

*Chapter Six*

# Disciples of Wainwright – Breakfast with the Wainwrights – A quibble about Wild Boar Fell – Afoot in Highland Scotland – A Morecambe panorama.

As sufferers from Wainwrightosis, Bob, Stan, Colin and I did not wish to be cured. Intoxicated by his writing style, and cheerfully following in his footsteps, we climbed all 214 of the fells he had mentioned in his first series of seven Lakeland guide books. We were inclined to jabber, to drink in views – also tepid tea – and to forever quote from AW's books.

A Pennine Journey (1986), relating to the long walk a badly-shod AW had undertaken in 1938, was a favourite. He quoted, as a prelude, lines from Ammon Wrigley, a noted Lancashire dialect writer:

> *And all I have writ is writ,*
> *Whether it be blest or curst.*
> *O remember the little that's good*
> *And forgive and forget the worst.*

Every page of the book had something that was wrily amusing. In Wharfedale, he "proceeded at a snail's pace up the green track, faithfully, adhering to all its zig-zags. At Muker, he knocked on the door of the first cottage, and it was opened by a woman who was wearing false teeth which were palpably new and untrained." Having set his camera for a time-exposure, he forgot to alter it back. "From Bowes to Blanchard, in Northumberland, the shutter of my camera was wide open."

My assault on the fells that were to be classified as "Wainwrights" began on 9 December, 1984, when I joined a small party including Michael, Bob's son, who at the

*Emblem of the Blunderers.*

*Bob and Colin, two of the Blunderers, on the flanks of Blencathra.*

*Bill and Bob, seated; Stan and Colin standing, with Great Gable as a backdrop.*

age of fourteen was knocking the last peak or two from the list. Bob recalls that I had some boots but, as far as he was aware, little fellwalking experience. At the end of a long and tiring walk, taking in several notable peaks, I presented Michael with two books about Lakeland.

I had been incinerating cigarettes by the yard. I stopped this habit, abruptly, to decarbonise my lungs. We were to become known as the Geriatric Blunderers' Walking Club. None of us was young and, like AW, we were ramblers with a distinctive (somewhat zany) character and behaviour. Betty Wainwright – dear Betty – became our President by dint of providing afternoon tea at her home at least once a year. Since AW's death, Betty had moved to smaller and more modern quarters at Burneside. She had always fancied living in a bungalow.

We cherished our friendship with Betty in her own right and because afternoon tea took place in a room decked with reminders of AW. These ranged from a large oil painting of landscape to a small bronze figure of AW, seated and sucking his pipe. On one amusing occasion, Bob greeted the diminutive Betty in a unique way. He picked her up, kissed her, then gently put her down again!

The extensive lounge had picture windows, the main ones giving a view of pleasant fields with an occasional rumbling passage of a Windermere-bound train. On our annual visits, Betty's catering was simple, local and adequate. We were never short of topics to discuss. Betty recalled her first meeting with AW in his office. It seems that she turned up to be reprimanded over some delayed payment for a travelling ballet company who had used the Town Hall for a performance. Instead of a crestfallen departure, Betty became his friend and also his chauffeur on his fell-seeking trips. He was able to continue his mission of documenting the fell-country.

Eventually, in what she described as a comfortable, loving companionship, she not only drove but walked with him until death robbed her (and us) of the characterful Mr Wainwright. She told us of their joint love for cats, mostly strays, via Animal Rescue, Cumbria, which was their special charity. A photograph we saw showed a serene AW, seat, pipe in hand, black and white cat on lap, and a smiling Betty, standing, one hand on a white cat. AW was not especially a doggy person, though his concern for the well-being of animals took in the canine variety.

We sent Betty copies of the reports of walks undertaken under the Geriatric Blunderers' auspices. She usually acknowledged them with a short note on Animal Rescue paper, featuring one of AW's distinctive drawings. Once, arriving at her home dripping wet, for yet another presidential afternoon tea, I asked I could dry off my notes in her oven or the notepaper would revert to mush.

The Blunderers were imaginative. Bob and I clambered out of our respective beds in the early hours and – while it was still dark – drove up the M6, heading for

*Betty Wainwright.*

*The head of a fine Herdwick Tup.*

Haweswater. We planned to watch the sun rise from the ridge leading up to High Street. Bob had spoken enthusiastically about the spectacle of a red sun flooding the area with red light, revealing red water, red hills, red sheep, even red deer.

Near Shap, the expedition nearly came undone when we were stopped by the police near Shap Summit. Their interest was not over a speeding offence. It was simply that ours was a lone vehicle, travelling fast. We were possibly up to no good. Bob opened the boot, which we had half filled with walking gear. A young constable asked if I [the driver] was the owner of the vehicle. The answer was in the affirmative. He then wanted to know our destination.

I gulped and in my reply hoped that the constable was a Lakelander with a romantic streak, for I said: "We're going to watch the sun rise from the head of Haweswater." He smiled – and waved us on. That morning, the sun did rise – as it had done for uncountable years – but it skulked behind cloud. We completed the walk along the ridge to the High Street plateau, where I sat with my back to a drystone wall, in drizzle, eating tomato sandwiches. Ugh.

Another time, we set off for Great Gable and arrived at the summit of Great End, which is marginally higher. It was Remembrance Day and we had hoped to join a throng at the head of Gable for a regular ceremony – the tooting of bugle and the customary two minutes of silence. The last time I had done this was in the company of a man and his dog which, standing on a nearby rock, spent two minutes licking my face.

Why, on this latest occasion, did we ascend the wrong peak? Overnight, there had been snow which became plated with ice. Parts of the M6 to Shap were slippery, to say the least. So were stretches of the road from the Penrith turn-off to Keswick. Yet it was still autumn. Trees were adorned with multi-toned leaves as well as snow, except by Derwentwater and into Borrowdale, where we encountered flooded areas.

The Honister road was blocked by snow. We continued to the dalehead, thence by upland trod and tarnside towards Great End. Conditions were alpine – snow and ice, now under a powder-blue sky. Lacking crampons, I slipped and fell several times. Where the coarse vegetation was draped with ice, and strummed by a breeze, there was a pleasant tinkling sound as slivers of ice that dangled from coarse vegetation jostled with each other over acres of ground. We arrived at the highest point just before 11 a.m and looked across a deep void to where a huddle of folk had gathered at the monument to remember the gallant dead.

Generally, our excursions were marked by classic fellwandering. We used the map rather than AW's guide. He was rarely out of our thoughts. If we came across a solitary metal gate, the wire of the fence having corroded, we checked it to see if it was still capable of swinging on its hinges. If so, it would be used.

Wainwright had been fascinated by gates. Like him, they were individualistic. He wrote: "There seem as many ways of fastening a gate as there are gates...No two are quite alike." We respectfully opened the Wainwright gate and before leaving ensured it had closed with a clang so the next gust of wind would not fling it free on its rusty hinges. Stan decreed that these gates should always be climbed. As he did so, he got some strange looks from other fellwalkers.

Some of AW's early excursions with his son Peter were into the limestone country just over the county boundary. On an April day in 1996, Bob, Colin and I, while exploring Langstrothdale, rejoiced that in bright light the pearl-white rock seemed to light up the landscape. We gained our operational height with a moderate climb from the parking place at Buckden. Bob commented on the ancient ash trees that grew from cracks in limestone. He had the impression the trees were wearing stone corsets!

Now the walking was pleasant – a level path, mainly green underfoot though with lots of rambler-flattened mole-heaps. Perhaps this route would be a little too popular for the likes of AW, for whom two was a crowd, though in his old age he would have appreciated the reasonably level ground. Four dark-toned ponies grazed near the felltop, which held the cores of old snowdrifts. A sign indicated the name of the tiny settlement of Cray. We slithered towards Kidstones Pass and the White Lion inn.

A farmer's wife was trying to train a dog that was still at a stage where it was flat and floppy. Her husband carried a sack containing sheep food. He had a crook at hand and a good dog at foot. There was just enough time to listen to his relevant story - of an old-time farmer at Oughtershaw who was nicknamed Tarzan. One day he shepherded by remote control. Looking over a wall, he shouted: "Get round, you begger. Get round, you begger." A visitor asked him if he was calling to the dog. "Nay," he relied, "it's wife."

The farmer entered a field and spread "ewe cobs with glucose", which were eagerly taken by his Dales-bred sheep with lambs at foot. Half a dozen lambs, which had been frolicking, were transfixed by the dog, which stood looking at them from a range of a few feet. Looking back, we saw Buckden Pike, grey-blue, dabbed with snow. A simple bridge spanned a narrow limestone gill which was temporarily dry.

The immediate area was decked by veteran ash trees, some of them held in a vice-like grip by outcropping rock. A green woodpecker (or yaffle) gave its laughing call, reminding me of the time when an old friend set up a pylon "hide" in the hillside wood near Hubberholme Church and allowed me to enter it, having a splendid view of the nesting hole of green woodpeckers.

Seen from a distance of a few feet, they looked as colourful as parrots. By maintaining a food supply for out-of-sight nestlings, I had time between feedings to make notes and change films. AW would have found the experience of being perched high above ground daunting. The wood used for the pylon was ancient stuff taken from a cottage being restored. The structure creaked ominously.

We passed through a different sort of wood, higher up the dale. The trees were uniformly thin and exceedingly tall – the equivalent of forced rhubarb. A curlew called. Years ago, before the dale-country meadows were transformed, the traditional haycrop being succeeded by early-to-harvest silage, the area would have been ringing with the calls of curlew and lapwing. Across the dale was Raisgill and the Horse Head Pass, leading over to Halton Gill in Littondale.

AW was fascinated by some of the old placenames. Yockenthwaite, in Langstrothdale – Yockenwhit to the natives – is an example. A visitor who asked a resident to spell it did not get an immediate answer. Then the local remarked: "Nay – it's not meant to be spelt; just said." We were on the Dales Way and signs conducted us down to the river side, where a merganser drake slumbered on a boulder. A dipper departed, quickly, purposefully, like a feathered dart.

We returned to the car park by the riverside path. At Hubberholme Church we searched for mice – carvings on the pews by Thompson of Kilburn – and heard that during the Great Flood of 1558 fish were found swimming within the building. A flash of blue along the river was a kingfisher in headlong flight. The doors on outside toilets at the George Inn, just across the river, still bore the dales-type signs – Tups and Yows, representing Men and Women.

Bob, whose business interests with Leeds Permanent Building Society caused him to flit from Lancaster to Kendal each Friday, had long been fascinated by Wainwright's writings. One morning, he courageously knocked on the door of the Wainwright residence on Kendal Green, half expecting a rebuff. Instead, AW had invited him in for a chat. As expected, the host was taciturn, a characteristic summed up in the Yorkshire Dales as the ability to say nowt for a long time.

Bob recalled that he had first met AW in 1979, two years after he had been in correspondence with him. "We moved to the north-west in 1978. I really wanted to meet him. Plucking up courage one day, I knocked at his door on Kendal Green. He himself answered the door. When I explained who I was, he said: 'You'd better come in.' Which was quite amazing. I sat down and had what amounted to a second breakfast. It was the first meal of many I had at the Wainwright home. The first thing that struck me about AW was that he was a big fellow. Over six foot. Betty was diminutive but she stood up to him all the time; there was no question about that. And he thought the world of her."

Bob did not foist himself on AW every week. It was roughly once a month, when he had business in Kendal. "I'd pop in there at about nine o'clock. I'd have some breakfast and Betty and I would put the world to rights. He was usually stuck in The Daily Telegraph."

Bob recalls the anguish he and his colleagues felt in that year, 1987. The Financial Services Act had come out the previous year. It was to lead to, among other things, the mass mis-selling of endowment policies. "A lot of us in the building society were fed up and wanted to get out. I went to see AW and he said to me, just off the cuff: 'Time you got out of that Building Society, Bob.'

"I knew exactly to what he was referring. I added that principles didn't pay the bills. He grunted and stuck his head back in the paper. Two years went by and I got an early retirement package. Calling at his house, I had some breakfast and then asked him if he remembered what he had said about the Financial Services Act. He said: 'Yes'. I said: 'I've just got an early retirement package.' He looked up, said 'Good' and stuck his head back in the Daily Telegraph."

Bob continued to visit him, though when he stopped work he did not often go into Kendal. AW became housebound. He got older and larger and slower. Betty still wanted to go out. Bob took her out seven or eight times. I joined them for one memorable walk based on Dent.

Gradually, over several years, Bob built up a correspondence with AW, who invariably replied promptly on a narrow folded card with one of his drawings on the front. It would be typed up longways and, always, was signed in green ink. An example followed an ascent of Wild Boar Fell, above Mallerstang. On May 21, 1977, when climbing this fell for the first time, with a Wainwright guide to hand, Bob noticed that AW had given the trig column number as 10797. The metal plate seen by Bob was inscribed 11810.

"I wrote to him, pointing out that he had got it wrong! I did not have long to wait for a reply. It was inconceivable that he was wrong. Had I been drunk?" Bob returned to Wild Boar Fell on March 2, 1978. "Sure enough my number was still there. I wrote once again to AW, having my small son Michael to back up my claim. For two years, I heard nothing. Then he wrote to me again. When contacting the Ordnance Survey with queries, AW had mentioned the mystery of Wild Boar Fell."

It turned out to be one of a number of tags filched by visitors as souvenirs. When the OS, on a routine visit, found one missing, it was replaced with the next available number in sequence. AW wrote to Bob: "We were both right!" (AW had, in fact, been informed of the re-numbering by another correspondent who had a similar experience to Bob and who, writing to the Ordnance Survey, had the situation explained.)

By the time he was fourteen years of age, Bob's son Michael had topped all Wainwright's 214 named peaks. When one peak remained, I was asked if I would like to join the ascent of Seat Sandal. Though woefully out of condition, I agreed. We left one vehicle in the car park beside the pub by Dunmail Raise and walked from a second car, which was brought to rest in the car park opposite the pub on Kirkstone Pass. The approach to Seat Sandal was Red Screes!

It was one of those near vertical climbs which a beginner is soon seeing in a red haze. I tottered by Little Hart Crag, Dove Crag, Hart Crag, and Fairfield. Following a steep descent and an-almost-as-steep ascent, I stood with Michael and the others on the summit of Seat Sandal. It was dusk. By the time we had reached the park where we had left the car, it was dark. We indulged in the unusual game of "find the car".

In 1984, Bob suggested to AW that they do a joint business venture to raise some money for Kepallan, the animal rescue charity. The basis of this was we were going to have 2,000 prints of five of his favourites from his Lakeland sketchbooks, which I was permitted to choose. They would be printed off to a pre-determined size to be framed and would be sold at £500 each. AW would sign each one and each would have a numbered certificate of authenticity on the back.

An enduring memory for Bob was of going up to AW's home on a Friday to collect another batch of these prints – probably 250 – each print signed in green ink and each written as meticulously as the previous one. "At the end of the day we had one, a larger size, and the problem was that it was going to cost too much to frame. Four such prints would take up a lot of space on someone's wall. I kept this one and decided to get it framed. But it hadn't got the annotation." Bob recalls that it was a study of the Langdale Pikes from Lingmoor.

"AW said he would put an annotation on and sign it for me. He took it upstairs and came down, looked at it, and said: 'I've made a mistake.' I couldn't believe that Wainwright would make a mistake. He said: 'I'll fix it.' AW took it back upstairs. "When he came down, I saw he had stuck some paper across and he had put the correct annotation. At first I was quite upset about this. Then I thought it was amazing. I was about to become, probably, the only person who had got anything from Wainwright on which there was a mistake."

Scotland came close to Lakeland in AW's affections. Lying to the north of Lakeland, beyond the sands and shimmering waters of the Solway Firth, and visible from the northern fells, were the blue hills of south-west Scotland. In 1936, while still living in a milltown setting, AW had a solo first trip north of the Border, chosing Arran, a handily placed island so large that it had a full range of scenery, from big, bare mountains in the north to an almost Irish pastoral landscape in the south, a few miles distant. Ireland, land of saints and shamrocks, might be seen in clear weather as a blue-grey smudge on the horizon.

He had a camera and his impressions of the island were to be jotted down alongside prints of his photographs. His first view of the island was from the pierhead at Ardrossan. On Arran, he climbed all the hills, waded in burns, lay on a heathered moor, and exalted in the views. He hinted at one of the glories of Arran. To him, the sun was touching it with a rosy radiance. He left the island feeling he had enjoyed something more than a holiday – a honeymoon perhaps. He was a lover torn from the arms of his bride.

I did not have to tear myself away from the arms of Freda, my wife, who never grumbled at my Blundering. The Blunderers being temporarily unavailable, I was accompanied by Fred, who also had a high regard for AW. At Ardrossan, we dined at an Indian Restaurant, where everyone spoke with a Scottish accent, and had an old Indian dish (mushroom omelette with chips).

At the time of year when few holidaymakers were astir, someone had dreamed of a fortnight's golfing festival. The ferryboat we joined had a contingent of women golfers. One of them would occupy the next bedroom to mine in the sea front hotel on Arran. She was not only an accomplished golfer but loved socialising, entertaining her friends in the bedroom till way beyond my bedtime – and then, asleep, snoring with such intensity I had a fancy that the intervening wall was shivering.

By day, Fred and I wandered between Cock of Arran and Bennan Head, the most northerly and southerly points of this astonishing island. They were a mere 19 miles apart. Striding along the northern road, we arrived in an area of jagged peaks that looked purple in dull light. Red stags grazed on quiet hillsides. Eiders were common at the sea's edge. The drakes maintained station like two-tone buoys. The dowdy ducks had new-hatched young, snug in black down, clustered behind them.

Just north of the Bay where we had our quarters stood Brodick Castle, the ancient seat of the Dukes of Hamilton and now the property of the National Trust for Scotland. Rising beyond the Castle was Goat Fell, a name which originally meant "windy hill". On a day when it was so calm that cigarette smoke hung about in the great outdoors, Fred and I decided to climb Goat Fell, the attic of Arran. It would be an honest climb from sea level to 2,866-ft.

Being the first visitors of the day, we contrived to become "lost" so that we might maintain a Yorkshire tradition and have a free inspection of the castle gardens. (Later, we discovered that there was no charge for entry to those gardens!) Our route to the summit lay through rhododendron grove, spruce plantation, birch belt, heather zone, expanses of coarse grass and eventually bare slopes strewn with boulders.

We were overtaken by half a dozen eager youngsters, members of a school party. We admired their enthusiasm until, at the summit, we discovered they were illicit cigarette smokers, far enough ahead of their teachers for their weakness to be undetected. I recall the descent as an ankle-ricking experience. It took us two hours to descend, along the knobbly dried-up bed of a burn. We had our first snack by the sea. Fred teased the eider drakes by imitating their crooning voice: "Ah-oo-ah". He said it was like the sound made by a duchess who had just had her bottom pinched.

Given good weather, AW – on that first Scottish visit – would have heard that Arran, his choice, was noted for its sunsets. Fred had a hankering to see such a spectacle. We switched from the premature dusk of Brodick, on the east coast, motoring to Mackrie. Static cloud was tethered to Kintyre but the sky beneath was clear and would soon be occupied by the orange-red orb of a setting sun.

The main hue was lemon, which coloured the sea. As the sun dipped, the landscape turned to gold. We decided to motor on to Lochranza, where the hills were aglow with a red tint from the almost-expired sun. (Curiously, the sky above was an icy blue.) The sunset glow on the hills, reflected in the water, had given the loch a bright red tint. We turned to find the dark clouds to the west liberally streaked as though they were bleeding.

A band of red lay over the clear purple hills of Kintyre. The open sea appeared to be aflame. Our last major impression of Arran – which we had already listed as a part of Scotland favoured by AW – was of a world populated by strange red creatures – red people, red sheep, red gulls.

Unlike Betty, AW was not an especially musical person but I like to think that as a Carlisle train left Oxenholme, or later, as Chauffeur Betty engaged the gearing of her little car, AW had the celebrated tune to Road to the Isles in mind. He found joy in exploring Sutherland, where lies the oldest and hardest rock in Europe and the lean northern lands extending to the verdant Spey Valley, backed by the Cairngorms. Here a visitor need not be surprised if a flake of snow settled on his nose in mid-summer. His excursions took in the isle of Skye and the Black Coolins.

AW visited Wild Scotland annually, in May and September, for over three decades. His camera blinked over a thousand times. Photographs that were professionally enlarged formed the basis of his mountain sketches. During the austere years following the 1939-45 war, as a solitary visitor, he had entrained at Oxenholme and in the sparsely-populated areas of the north-west Scottish mainland used an occasional bus service. Miss one bus – and you might have to wait twenty-four hours for the next.

I was lured to Durness and the grandeur of Sutherland but was less enthusiastic about it than AW. In one of the BBC films, the now plump and elderly fellwanderer was more inclined towards roadwandering. Inland, in austere Sutherland, the last phase of glaciation might have occurred the day before yesterday. Here stood big bens, highpoints of the "knob and lochan" country, and themselves humbled by glacial ice, by wind, rain and frost. Like AW, I looked with admiration at the eroded stumps of what had been much nobler mountains. Elsewhere the landscape appeared to have sunk, or at least to be awash. Lochans, bogs and moorland, the bogs tufty with cotton sedge, the moors ribbed by peat workings: this was the lowland part of the county.

The name Sutherland is derived from a Norse source meaning "the South land" – south in relation to the northern isles which land-hungry Norsemen had overrun, their names becoming the language of topograpghy. There is Tongue, from tunga, meaning a tongue of land, and Eriboll, from eyrr bol, or Beach Town.  Durness is "the point of the wild beast" and Inchard is "the meadow loch." Laxford is derved from lax, or salmon.

Between the modest hamlet of Rhiconich and Durness, on the north coast, lay thirteen miles of travel through an acid wilderness that had been AW's promised land. At Durness, the landscape suddenly brightened. It was not just the effect of light reflected by the sea but the occurrence of limestone, a sweet filling in the dark geological sandwich of the north-west. Drystone dykes [walls made without mortar] gleamed in the afternoon sunlight, bordering fields of sappy grass – the sort of farming I knew and not traditional crofting.

The grass was scarcely tall enough to conceal a sparrow, but marsh marigolds flowered in the ditches, mountain avens covered rocky places, and the best land held a constellation of daisies. A pair of greenshank resided in a swampy hollow a mere five

*The Cairngorms from near Glenmore.*

*Page 80: Droman, Sutherland.*

*Page 81: Peat diggings near Durness, Sutherland.*

minutes walk from the hotel at Balnekeil, where I was to stay. Corncrakes return in May, when yellow iris provides the birds with cover until the development of the spring flush of vegetation.

AW was an animal lover. He was partial to dogs and sheep. I never rated him as a bird-watcher and wondered if, at Durness, on one of his Maytime trips, he listened to the rasping voice of the corncrake, now one of Britain's rarest birds. In my case, the local corncrake gave voice at intervals of from two to five minutes, from 2 p.m to 3 p.m.

In a spell of an hour and a half, the bird moved a mere thirty yards, crossing a tumbled wall. When walking, it resembled a chicken, keeping its head down, stopping periodically to maintain a fixed position, then – chicken-like – lunging to collect insects from the flower heads. Then, after standing as smartly as a guardsman, head up, neck outstretched, it cocked its head, tuning in to bird calls round about.

Faraid Head had about it a feeling of being the ultimate point. I crossed a desert zone – an area of shifting sand – leading to a headland where the blocky rocks might have been squared up by a quarryman. This hot Scottish desert was given a touch of life by wheatears that chacked and whistled. At the tip of the headland, kittiwakes shouted their names and shags sat morosely on their nests, some of which had been freshly adorned with greenstuff brought from the sea.

All the time I was at Durness, I had in mind Cape Wrath, "the turning point" of Norse seafarers.

AW and Eric Robson visited Cape Wrath courtesy of the BBC. We were informed in the commentary to a film that hereabouts the Norsemen directed their longboats, with the dragonesque prows, southwards to the Hebrides. AW exalted at the sight of the mighty Atlantic breaking its back against dark cliffs; Eric mentioned that the lighthouse had been built by the Stevenson family, one of whom was the author Robert Louis Stevenson.

I waited near the Cape Wrath Hotel for the small, white-painted ferry boat, with outboard engine attached, that in the 1980s, the time of my visit, voyaged confidently at flow tide, picking its way around sandbanks at half-tide and was laid up at the ebb. The mini-bus I saw on the far shore had been taken across the water on a special raft. During my crossing we were in the company of eiders – those big, blunt-looking ducks – that were towing rafts of downy young.

A road eleven miles long terminated with the lighthouse. AW and Eric Robson stood where the Lewisian gneiss had its final grand flourish. On my visit, I preferred the adjacent 600-ft cliffs of Torridonian sandstone, which are tonally much warmer and have been weathered to the stage where ledges provide nesting spaces for a host of

*Eric Robson, a companion of AW on BBC documentaries.*

*Page 84: Near Cape Wrath.*

seabirds, notably kittiwakes and razorbills. Puffins burrow on steep grassy banks. The many offshore stacks, remnants of the old coastline, being also of sandstone, should have had a reddish hue. They had been plastered with seabird droppings and resembled ice cakes.

AW left his footprints on a remote and lovely crescent-shaped beach known as Sandwood Bay and, with it, a remnant pinnacle, known as The Herdsman. To AW, the best sounds were natural sounds, preferably silence. He could concentrate on his photography. In the six sketchbooks he compiled about wildest Scotland are incorporated about 400 Scottish mountain drawings.

When I wrote a light-hearted book about adventuring in Scotland with three pals, under the title It's a Long Way to Muckle Flugga, AW kindly provided a foreword. I visited him to discuss the project. Betty provided a cup of tea. A visiting printer was left to explore the garden. AW's only reservation about the book was its title. Muckle Flugga? Some potential readers might imagine, from the sound of Muckle Flugga, that this far northern sea-washed lump with a lighthouse, off Unst, Shetland, might be in Ireland. Wisely, I added a sub-title to the book: "Journeys in northern Scotland."

My book had been inspired by words written by Felix Mendelssohn, composer, who with a friend had toured wildest Scotland in 1829. Mendelssohn confided in his diary: "...it is no wonder that the Highlands have been called melancholy. But two fellows have wandered through them, laughed at every opportunity, rhymed and sketched together, growled at one another and at the world if they happened to be vexed or found nothing to eat, devoured everything in sight when they did find it and slept 12 hours every night. These two were we – and we'll not forget it as long as we live..."

In the foreword to my Muckle Flugga book, AW wrote about me in fulsome terms, adding: "He has long had a love affair with the remote places of the Highlands and Islands of Scotland, travelling not as a tourist but as a nomadic wanderer inspired by a special interest in the ornithology and the fauna and flora of these lonely regions. In this pleasant volume he recalls many of his adventures and explorations and discoveries that remain fresh in his memory and tells of them in an entertaining and often amusing style.

"Manifest through the pages is his consuming interest in the natural life and scenery of the crofting communities and wilderness areas of the western seaboard and its mountainous hinterland. This is an enjoyable account of his travels, and will appeal not only to those who have an affinity with the places he describes so well but also to others who like to sit in an armchair with a jolly good book."

I told AW I proposed to dedicate the book to three lively, outdoor-minded grandchildren: Helen, Kathryn and Gillian. And that whenever I thought of the wild Atlantic coast of Scotland, Mendelssohn's Hebrides Overture came to mind. We

c/o Westmorland Gazette,
KENDAL, Cumbria,
27th September 1975

Dear Mr Green,

Thankyou for your reminder. I expect to be able to let you have
Aonach Eagach quite early next summer. I have just got Volume Two off to
the printer, having been delayed for more than a year by a desire to do a
sort of requiem for dear-departed Westmorland, which too is now finished,
so that I am ready for Volume Three and rarin' to start, although, as I think
I told you, the drawing of A.E. and a few others are already done. In two
weeks time, I go up to Glencoe to finish off the fieldwork for that area.
I go there in some apprehension, actually, having booked a caravan in Glencoe
and being unaccustomed to this type of accommodation. But hotel charges are
really getting out of hand. I shall know later whether the suffering is worth
the saving.

You are obviously a good deal tougher than I am. How often have I
looked up lingeringly at A.E. and An Teallach and Liathach and the rest and
how much I have read of their terrors for the timid pedestrian, and how often
I have turned sadly away. I am getting old. I like a clear and easy path.

I will be in touch in a few months if I survive the caravan.

Yours sincerely.
A.Wainwright

*Letter from AW to a postal admirer in September 1975, signed in his customary green ink.*

associate it in particular with Fingal's Cave, on the island of Staffa, with its striking
hexagonal basaltic columns.

Among a host of Scottish letters AW received in the summer of 1974 was one from a
Mr Green. AW's reply, headed c/o The Westmorland Gazette, Kendal, had become
lodged in a book that a friend of mine bought second-hand. Pleasure was expressed at
hearing from Mr Green again. AW congratulated him on his successful assault on the
Aonach Eagach ridge, "an object I have had my sights on for donkeys years but never
ventured to attempt. I have grown old looking at it from a safe distance and now the
effort is beyond me. You are one up on me there, all right!"

AW had already drawn the mountain in advance for his third volume of Scottish
drawings, "which means, as the first is only now being printed, a wait of another two
years. You can have it, with pleasure, when it becomes available. Since my memory,
like my legs, is no longer capable of sustained effort, I beg of you to remind me nearer
the time. There are still stirrings of life in me."

In June, he had climbed two Munro's in the Glen Affric area. "Easy ones. Nothing
like Aonach Eagach. You must be a proud man. I would be, if I were in your boots."
AW signed the letter, as usual, using green ink. In the autumn of 1975, AW reported
to his postal admirer that "I expect to be able to let you have Aonach Eagach quite

early next summer." He had just got Volume Two off to the printer, "having been delayed for more than a year by a desire to do a sort of requiem for dear-departed Westmorland, which too is now finished, so that I am ready for Volume Three and rarin' to start…"

In a fortnight's time, he would be driven to Glencoe to finish off the fieldwork for that area. "I go there in some apprehension, actually, having booked a caravan in Glencoe and being unaccustomed to this type of accommodation. But hotel charges are really getting out of hand. I shall know later whether the suffering is worth the saving."

He concluded: "You are obviously a good deal tougher than I am. How often have I looked up lingeringly at A.E and An Teallach and Liathach and the rest and how much I have read of their terrors for the timid pedestrian, and how often I have turned sadly away. I am getting old. I like a clear and easy path. I will be in touch in a few months if I survive the caravan."

For many years, AW and Betty travelled to Scotland with Harry Firth, who by now, after many years of an editor-printer relationship, was an old friend of mine. In the car, on the Road to the Highlands and the Isles, were AW, Betty, Harry (the driver) and his wife Kay. AW said little. They were noticeably silent journeys. At an overnight hotel, AW would either be eating, poring over a map or, in his bedroom, planning the next day's exertions.

On other trips North of the Border, the chauffeur would be Betty, with AW as the only passenger. A whiff of Scottish air became an annual necessity. I dare not ask AW if, on Scottish jaunts, he occasionally exchanged his beloved fish and chips for haggis and chips. Six books of Scottish Mountain Drawings were compiled between 1974 and 1979.

In June, 1996, we Blunderers, drawn back to Scotland by AW's enthusiasm for the hill country, spent several days in swirling cloud, mist, rainstorms full of spite and (now and again) bits of blue – enough to patch a Dutchman's trews. We arrived just before the Midge Season. The weather was at its sunniest, warmest, clearest best as we drove home!

Lochside woods were adorned by new leaf, bluebells and bracken. AW disliked Gaelic names for mountains. Bob practised his "Garlic", as it applies to some of them. The sounds from his throat were like the grating of car gears. North of Lomond, we were in the real Scotland – big bens, bottle-green pines, yellow-flowering broom, wee lassies, wee wifeys, bothies, neaps (turnips) and tatties (spuds). At Crianlarich we passed the imaginary line crossing Scotland – a line that separates the Potato Line – to the south, chipped; to the north – mashed!

Next morning, we awoke in our lodgings at Tyndrum to find it was dull, misty, with improved humidity - about 70 per cent. On the bird table, siskins were fratching over peanuts. Breakfast was English style, plus Scotch pancake and black pudding – which is why, at the end of the holiday, despite strenuous exercise on the hills, each of us put on about half a stone. The proprietress said: "It's still raining. They said it would take up. They said the same last week. It didn't."

At Crianlarich, Colin saw "a chink", then the much rarer "blue patch". The Dochart falls at Killin had responded to heavy rain. Colin drove us on the high road to Ben Lawers information centre, where we gleefully toured an exhibition without paying – and then realised we would have to pay at the exit. We took the path leading to the Ben. On Beinn Ghlas, over 2,500-ft above the Killin bakery, we feel a little smug at having done the climb in two hours.

The mist dispersed. Now all was revealed with clarity and colour. Six hundred feet of climbing on an unstable slope culminated in an effort to stand up in a brisk wind at trig point 51510, a pimple on the face of Ben Lawers, the ninth highest hill in aw Scutland.

Next day we plodged across part of the soggy wilderness of Rannoch Moor. We boarded the 10-17 a.m train from Upper Tyndrum to Corrour, where I inquired if this was the station for the Middle of Nowhere, to be told: "Och yes – and it's near to heaven." Bob whispered: "It's warmer in Hell." The railway station was at an elevation of 1,350-ft. Ramblers shuffled off into the murk. We stayed behind a while, anxious to have this famous stretch of the Road to the Isles (twixt Tummel and Lochaber) to ourselves.

I stalked a fine eight-pointer stag. When I was about 10 yards from it, and had come under its unblinking stare, I realised this beasty could hardly be termed "wild". Two folk appeared from the Youth Hostel by Loch Ossian. One of them shouted: "Windswept", which turned out to be a nickname for the stag. Four other fine deer habitually frequent the hostel. They were said to eat anything, from bread to Mars bars.

We took the tacky road from the Isles (as did the cattle being taken on the hoof along this famous drove road). Clouds played hide and seek on the hills that rose from the wilderness, the resort of a few pairs of golden plover and the celebrated Rannoch red deer, which reputedly have webbed feet. These were not often seen. The beasts are

*Over: Lochs on Rannoch Moor.*

invariably standing in water.

We arrived, at 1,750-ft, by what remains of an old shooting lodge that subsequently became an isolation hospital. Bob fancied it was a desert fort. We elevated its status to "buttying place" – and promptly broached our lunch-bags. And, lo, the rain stopped. We de-breeked – the waterproof breeks, that is – and rejoiced in seeing once again the blue remembered hills.

The Grandmother of All Rainstorms was already smudging the north-western horizon. We were enveloped by another sheet of wetness. By the time we quit the moor, we had reached the couldn't-care-less stage and ceased to worry about keeping dry. The new road seemed to be tilted, as though it was installed on the drip-dry principle. We hastened to Rannoch Station. The refreshment room was open, despite a prior lack of customers. As we drank and ate, the proprietress ran a mop over the floor to absorb the water that had dripped from our clothes.

Determined to have some bright memories, we booked passage from Oban to Mull and from Mull to Staffa. The boat breasted an uneasy green sea, smacking the water, sending up sheets of spray. As we neared the island, composed of lava that cooled into mainly hexagonal columns, almost everyone must have been bringing to mind the strains of Mendelssohn's musical appreciation of this coastline. Bob, walking on a line of basaltic rocks towards the Cave, simply remarked on passing me: "Magic!"

AW being on our minds for most of the time we spent on that Scottish holiday, it was imperative to find a Munro we could climb. In the end, it was decided to leave the car at Bridge of Orchy and tackle Beinn Dorain and Beinn an Dothaidh (do your best with the pronunciation). The climb to the bealach, between awesome peaks, was unremitting and muddy.

On Ben Dorain, we met a "proper Scotsman". He sported a thick red beard, as do all proper mountaineers. In conversation, he turned out to be Scottish-Yorkshire. His father was a Scotsman and his mother had been brought up at Addingham, near Skipton. He had nine Munros to go on his third circuit of the high tops. A man after AW's lungs!

The ascent of Beinn an Dothaidh was just a hard slog, with nothing much to see en route except a man from Deep South who came up each year for six weeks to compile a treatise on moraines. We reckoned it was really to escape from Watford and his wife. From the rim of the peak we felt we could survey half of Scotland. Ben Nevis presided on the skyline. A nearby peak, which looked diminutive, was said to have an elevation of over 4,000-ft. Below was the soggy Moor of Rannoch.

Back in the Lake District, with Freda my wife, I joined the many guests at the Wild Boar Hotel, twixt Kendal and Windermere, in June, 1982, to honour Harry Firth on his retirement from the Westmorland Gazette. As the event was about to start, AW was ushered in by Betty. Seats at the top table awaited them. He, who did not care much for social occasions, was making a special effort for the man who had nurtured his publishing ambitions from the earliest time to success and fame.

Years later, Bob suggested to AW that he consider another commercial venture: the view from Morecambe Promenade from what is known as the Stone Jetty, which is where the train used to cross from the railway station to the steamers. Yes, he would consider it if he could do it in black and white. Bob, using a camera and a tripod, took upwards of 50 photographs in black and white, all the way round.

"I pasted them all together. I showed them to him and he said, in that rich, deep voice of his: 'Your photography is not very good, Bob.' I was a bit chewed off about this. I prided myself on my photography. Betty looked over and said: 'It's not his photography; it's your eyes'." She took him off to the optician. And that's when he found he had got macular degeneration. A development from all the close work he had undertaken with his drawings. It's rather sad. That scheme never came to anything.

His speech was almost staccato. A man of very few words. He could sometimes be off-hand with people. On one occasion I was at AW's house when another visitor arrived; he made the newcomer wait on the doorstep till I had left. Andrew, his printing manager, was permitted to knock and immediately enter.

He never had a wrong word with Betty, though she could be firm with him at times when firmness would be his friend. She was the one who took him in hand during the Kendal years when he was living on not much more than fish and chips. He got double pneumonia. Betty, a retired nurse, arranged for him to be admitted into the old Kendal Green hospital, which was on the doorstep. She would go in and look after him; she nursed him back to health.

The Blunderers revered AW. Bob completed the 214 Wainwrights on Allen Crags; Stan ticked off the last Wainwright on Red Pike, Wasdale; he was photographed atop the fell, sitting on a natural stone chair. Colin's last peak was Fleetwith Pike. I settled for Lingmell.

## Chapter Seven

# The Blunderers undertake AW's Coast to Coast from St Bees, against the grain of the landscape to Robin Hood's Bay.

The Blunderers organised at least one walk, of a week's duration, each year. We split the Coast to Coast Walk, among the most popular of AW's creations, into two parts. We walked from west to east. Dividing the experience into two parts was necessary to allow me to have a heart operation in Leeds Infirmary, with time to recover before donning boots for the eastern phase.

The Coast to Coast put the Pennine Way to shame for scenic beauty, variety and interest. Walking with the wind, four of us crossed Lakeland, the Vale of York and North York Moors. The western part, involving 12,000-ft of climbing, was undertaken in May, 1994 . AW was in our minds for most of the time we were a-foot. Someone wrote there is no day in the Lakeland week that might properly be called Sun-day. The conditions for the walk were exceptional. The sun beamed on us from a cloudless sky.

For this expedition, each of us had a special part to play. Colin was the Organiser and Bob agreed to be Stills Photographer (who ran out of film after 45 minutes). Stan, the most handsome of the group, complete with beard, was appointed Duty Foreground (Photographic Section). I was classified as Videoist, Diarist, Tea-maker and OAP.

We converged on Hartley, near Kirkby Stephen, intending the use the Packhorse facility – a mini-bus – to move the heaviest items of our gear from place to place. There was much talk of notable Coast to Coasters. I heard of a luckless Dutch lady who had to retire when she was but a few yards into the adventure. She had tripped and broke a bone in a leg. An American couple who intended to celebrate their golden wedding looking for orang-utans in Borneo had opted for a Coast to Coast safari – and viewed a million hill sheep.

At St Bees, in true Blunderers' tradition, we spent the first half-hour sipping tea in a local restaurant. A Wainwright ritual was performed. We waded ankle deep in the Irish Sea and collected pebbles for deposition at Robin Hood's Bay. A lively tide soon re-arranged the beach. A schoolteacher who was collecting seaweed as a fertiliser for asparagus – a most unusual occupation – was persuaded to take group photographs at

*Metallic packhorse serving
Wainwright's Coast to Coast
Walk.*

the sea's edge.

The eroded path we followed edged the redstone cliffs. Our companions were herring
gulls, with laughing cries, and fulmar petrels, silently sail-planing. We walked beside
patches of sea pinks and bluebells. Bob, having just read a leaflet about National
Bluebell Week, informed us in grave tones that bluebells are a predominantly western
seaboard plant. We were reminded of Wainwright's dictum that a first-time rambler
needs to distinguish between a ripe bilberry and sheep droppings.

Irritatingly, for two whole miles, we walked in a direction that led us away from our
destination. It was a joyful moment when we turned eastwards. In sight were the
western outliers of Lakeland, including a huge hump of a fell known simply as Dent.
Hedges and trees were leafing-up. A yellow hammer uttered its "little-bit-of-bread-
and-no-cheese" ditty. We walked through a dandelion-yellowed field to the
unmemorable village of Moor Row.

The village of Cleater was a testing place for Coast to Coasters without a sense of direction. Four Dutch walkers, heading for Rosthwaite, were misdirected into Wasdale and had to struggle over Sty Head. A world record time for the first leg of the fourteen-mile walk from St Bees to Ennerdale Bridge was established by a man who consistently took wrong turnings and needed twelve hours for the journey. At a guest-house in Ennerdale Bridge, he was given a Megga-Wally award.

Wainwright's directions led us from Cleator on a long drag to the summit of Dent (1,100-ft), followed by a sharp, knee-cracking descent into Nannycatch Gate, a secluded Exmoor-like beauty spot. We passed near a stone circle which was modern – a Victorian sham. At Ennerdale Bridge, our quarters for the night were in a large, detached house with a shrubby, cat-haunted garden and a grid at the entrance to the grounds to protect it from footloose farm stock.

The proprietor – a raconteur – made a special award to some of his guests. The Cream Tissue Award was for those mean-minded folk who departed with the entire stock of tissues. The award had also been handed to the family who, discovering the airing cupboard, normally out of bounds, had managed to use up the entire reserve of towels during a short stay.

There were titters when we heard that some visitors who believed they were using a guide book had been carrying a coffee-table version of the Coast to Coast book, two-thirds of the illustrations being coloured pictures. They had been looking for a bank at a place named Dent. He gently pointed out that Dent is – a hill!

On the following day, there was a bright golden haze on the meadows. An impatient sun seemed to leap into the sky. The big fells around Ennerdale stood in various shades of blue and grey. There was a sparkle on t'watter. As we strode towards Ennerdale Water, a cuckoo called and, this being the first cuckoo heard by us this year, we turned over the money in our pockets – for luck!

A blissful, cuckoo-punctuated morning was spent striding along the western shore of the lake, which a dam has transformed into a very pretty reservoir. A cock ring ouzel uttered its cold, clear notes from a birch tree standing in a shadowy recess of Anglers' Crag. A passing raven saluted us by flicking momentarily on to its back.

As we approached the Irish Bridge – water flows both over and under it – we saw a greylag gander and presumed its mate was nesting nearby. The gee-whiz country, dominated by Gable and Pillar, was near at hand, but first we must slog through Forestry Commission plantations. Bob thought it appropriate to include a visit to Haystacks, via Scarth Gap, to pay homage to AW, founder of the walk we were now enjoying.

His ashes were scattered by Innominate Tarn (The Nameless One). Someone had

*The Blunderers pause to pay homage to AW on Haystacks.*

suggested linking it by name with Wainwright, but even he would not have been pleased at such a change. AW wrote that "the ascent of Haystacks via the pass of Scarth Gap is a prelude of much merit and beauty to a mountain walk of unique character...Save it, however, for a fine clear day."

So bright was the day, and so deep the blue of the Tarn, we had an impression that someone had poured Stephen's ink into it. Bob gave a touching little oration. In our top-of-the-world position, we were in the company of some Lakeland giants – Brandreth, Green and Great Gables, Scafell Pike, Kirk Fell and Pillar. The most optimistic of us remarked that the journey was now downhill all the way to Borrowdale – which, of course, this being the Lake District, it wasn't.

We strode on to Dub's Quarry, inspecting the (vandalised) interior of the "hut", where the only usable object was a tin of beans. The line of the old cable was our route to the Drum House, thence down the hill to Honister and Rosthwaite, where we had arranged to spend the night. At breakfast-time, we heard about a cockatoo that commuted between the house and the local inn.

We prepared for the morning assault on Greenup Gill and Lining Crag, attaining the skyline at 2,000-ft. Coast to Coasters were streaming up the hill like Klondykers. Bob had planned a route that avoided Grasmere, keeping to higher ground. We crossed from Steel Fell to Raise Beck falls across the top of Dunmail Raise. There was a novel view of Thirlmere and its flanking fells. Looking down, down, down, we saw a buzzard circling. Distantly, it looked like a brown moth.

Descending to road level was an ankle-wracking experience. We were in the realm of Herdwick sheep and their little dark lambs. AW was fascinated by hill sheep, which were among the first fell-walkers. He was deeply moved by the plight of straying or abandoned animals and admired the fortitude of Herdwicks, the native fell-going sheep which, during his walks, were his only companions. AW wrote: "They had an uncomplaining acceptance of the conditions in which they lived – out in dreadful weather all the time."

We crossed Dunmail Raise for the ascent to Grizedale Tarn. Beyond the many splendid waterfalls lay what we used to think of as Copydex Country, with the peat churned up by boots into a porridge-like mush. We rested near the Brothers Parting Stone at which William Wordsworth had bid what turned out to be his last farewell of John, a mariner, who soon was drowned at sea.

The path down Grizedale led to the park-like estate of Patterdale Hall, with its mighty walls and exotic trees rising in some cases to over 100-ft. A final saunter and we were at Greenbank Farm, having that day walked 16 miles and climbed a total of 3,500-ft. Phew!

Next day, we took the Angle Tarn track from Patterdale. Discovering we were only
60-ft from the summit of The Knott (2,424-ft) we trotted blithely to the summit cairn
– in case it was decided to "do the Wainwrights" again. The east wind was of the lazy
variety, determined to blow through a walker rather than taking the trouble to go
round. We clawed our way to the highest point of the Coast to Coast at Kidsty Pike
(2,560-ft).

The path along the western shore of Haweswater had almost as many ups and downs
as a hotel lift, passing Castle Crag, a hill fort at 1,300-ft and resting at Measand, where
many waterfalls tumbled into a gorge adorned by newly-leafed birch and alder. Gorse
was in bloom. That night, the chosen inn had an all-pervading tang of cigarette smoke.
Whenever a sleeper moved, an Alsatian barked.

After the high hills, we traversed a well-farmed landscape. Fields were thronged by
livestock. In waste places, prime clumps of marsh marigolds almost shouted to be
noticed. Shady places had a carpet of wood anemones. We were pilgrims for an hour
at the remains of Shap Abbey, the only abbey in Old Westmorland. Shap was our
"watering hole", with tea and big sandwiches featuring crab and mayonaisse.

The Coast to Coast crossed the Lancaster-Carlisle railway by a footbridge. Another
spanned the six lanes of the M6. Beyond lay limestone country. The scenery was being
shifted by quarrymen, using titanic vehicles to transport lumps of rock across a special
motorway bridge to crusher and kilns. On Crosby Ravensworth Fell we were on part
of the huge Westmorland Plateau. During this stage of the Coast to Coast, which Bob
humorously referred to as "seven miles of nowt", we inspected a 17th century
monument commemorating a halting place of a Royal Army.

With the long, featureless area traversed, we slipped down the hill to Orton. Beyond,
Sunbiggin Tarn, with its profusion of nesting gulls, gave a desolate area a sense of life.
At a farm near Sunbiggin Tarn, an old farmer we met sitting beside a barn passed his
time talking to Coast to Coasters. He had lost his dog. "I've heard it – but not seen it
for ages."

After some blundering, we reached Greenriggs farmyard, to be greeted (loudly and
angrily) by a dog attached to a kennel on which had been fixed the yellow arrow
marking the footpath. Our new quarters were at the Black Bull. At Kirkby Stephen,
roughly half way, we dined at the Coast to Coast fish and chip shop. A photograph of
AW adorned a wall in the dining area.

Part of my training for the western half of the Coast to Coast Walk was dining at this
fish-and-chippery, a type of establishment known to AW, from his boyhood days, as
a "chip shop". He was partial to this deep-fried, crisp, hot and golden fare. I had pressed
my nose against the glass panel of the door as the proprietor, Graham Pollitt, was
"rumbling". He was not suffering from a debilitating intestinal complaint but using a

mechanical system to remove the jackets from taties without recourse to a knife.

My companion was Nigel Holmes, of Radio Cumbria. At Appleby station I had recorded a five minute talk about Bishop Eric Treacy and his association with the Settle-Carlisle railway. Having had West Riding of Yorkshire incumbencies, I am sure that Eric Treacy had been "partial" to fish and chips. Nigel and I drove into Kirkby Stephen for yet another item for his Saturday morning programme.

My regard for fish and chips dates back to the 1930s, when it was possible to get a generous helping of both for thruppence. In days before vegetable oils were used, hunks of melting dripping floated in the pans like mini-icebergs. On a frosty night, eating fish and chips from paper, outdoors, meant that surplus fat trickled between the fingers and congealed. It was undoubtedly a sensation known to AW in his native Blackburn.

A notice on the door at Kirkby Stephen referred to the Coast to Coast Walk. Wainwright was pictured, seated, in silhouette, pipe in mouth, his gaze permanently on the chip pan.

In later life, his friends knew that one way to gain his regard was to drive him to a fish and chip shop, preferably in a palatial setting, such as Harry Ramsden's establishment at Guiseley.

The Blackburn lad, to whom the Lake District was heaven, never forgot his native milltown. He listed fish and chips among his favourite foods. As related, when Sue Lawley interviewed him on the radio for Desert Island Discs he asked, plaintively: "Will there be a chippy on the island?"

While watching a video composed of BBC films of the Coast to Coast Walk, I noticed that Wainwright, strolling down what is virtually the only street in Kirkby Stephen, appeared to be a little restive, doubtless being tantalised by an aroma compounded of fish, chips and mushy peas, sprinkled with vinegar.

Had one of the filmsters said: "Cut to chippery"? The two happy wanderers, Eric and AW, were now shown guzzling. The finished film gave no indication that the two diners had company – the cameraman, a sound engineer, the director, a girl with pad of paper and poised ballpoint pen – and goodness knows who else.

In those days, Frank Murray presided over the shop. Subsequently, everyone who ate their fish and chips on the premises asked to sit "where Wainwright had his fish and chips." When I called, in 1994, this was no longer possible. The table was moved into the main shop, where it supported the appliance that heated up the mushy peas, gravy and curry in their separate compartments. AW looked down on diners from a framed photograph that was taken by Kenneth Shepherd of Kendal.

Our Coast to Coasting was resumed. Up, up, up – from Hartley, near Kirkby Stephen,

*Framed photograph of AW in the fish and chip shop at Kirkby Stephen.*

to the summit of Nine Standards Rigg, with its profusion of cairns and a mountain
indicator provided by the local Mountain Rescue team and unveiled by – me! Stan
described the Nine Standards as "a very impressive blot on the landscape." Wooden
signposts and short posts tipped with yellow paint marked the way across Coghill Hill
(yes, double use of the word hill). We descended to Whitsun Dale, a long, strangely
empty valley in which the first habitation had the picturesque name of Raven Seat.

At Keld, we had cups of tea while sitting outside a farmhouse. Four walkers from
Sussex appeared. A limping man stripped off a sock to reveal blisters growing on
blisters. The best remedy, he affirms, was Germaline, covered with lambs-wool. His
wife, small but usefully stock, had the heaviest load. Stan, duty comedian, requested
her to shoulder her huge rucksack and walk away. She obliged, then turned to inquire
why he had requested this? Said Stan: "I've never seen a rucksack with legs afore."

In May, 1995, we undertook the eastern section of the Coast to Coast – from Keld to
Robin Hood's Bay, leaving a familiar Pennine landscape at Richmond for the Plain of
York, the fatty heartland of Yorkshire, and then coming to grips with the North York
Moors, which are thatched by a hundred thousand acres (40,000 ha) of bonnie heather.

This section began where the first had ended – at Keld, head of Swaledale, situated in the upper Dale Country at its best. We heard the contralto voices of ewes and the soprano cries of their new offspring. Keld is a Norse word meaning a spring. AW had written: "Always at Keld there is the music of the river." Also the hiss of water coursing down mossy rockfaces.

We strode down t'lonnin [lane], ower t'brigg [bridge] and up a brant [steep] hillside until I was "back o' Kisdon Hill", beholding the ruins of Crackpot Hall, the name crackpot derived from "crow cave". At Swinnergill, the calm air shivered from the hard, clear notes of the ring ouzel, our north country nightingale, as also from the scrapy calls of cock wheatears. Wrens, perched on the ruins of mine buildings, contributed arias of operatic power and quality.

At buttying-time [halt for food] we had a competition to identify the substance that came to view when Stan ripped open a foil-covered snack. Colin thought it resembled fishing bait. Bob was sure it was plastic chewing gum. Stan referred to it as a chocolate-covered snack. A moorland track led us to the head of Gunnerside Gill where – though the month of May was not out – a young woman in another party of walkers had cast several clouts and was soaking up the sunshine.

The Coast to Coast crossed over a blighted tract of moorland to Old Gang, where the chimney of a ruined smelt mill stood with the visual impact of an exclamation mark. Colin and I stopped to examine the remains of a hilltop peat-store at Old Gang mine. Bob and Stan, as straight-necked as fell foxes being hunted, kept walking and were soon lost to sight.

Near Surrender Mill, in what was now Herriot Country, swathed in mist, they headed for an ice cream van that proved to be a mirage. With Colin, I crossed a tract of moorland where we were stalked by a red grouse! We then took the riverside path from Healaugh to Reeth. The village was untypically noisy. AW, with his fondness for Blackburn Rovers, would have been elated to know that the local football team had won t'cup. He would have been less pleased at the revelry, which included draining t'cup of ale and a few "shorts". Each refill cost about £20.

After bed and breakfast in Reeth, we took a flagged path towards Grinton, where I concentrated so hard on videoing I fell, broke my specs and had a literally bleeding gash above one eye. The expedition foundered for an hour or so while we bought some special glue for the specs and Elastoplast for the wound. The doctor neatly reversed the process, using glue to seal the wound and Elastoplast to mend the specs.

On to Marrick Priory, now used as an outdoor centre. Marrick was a nunnery. The nun's flagged route through a local wood to the high-lying village of Marrick was a change from austere open country. The wood was floriferous. Glades held drifts of bluebells. Primroses and wood anemones were common. At Marsett, we detected a

certain stiffness towards Coast to Coasters by local folk doubtless sick to death of their
peerings and and questionings. The owner of an old chapel had a notice on the door
explaining its new status as a  private home.

We strode through a succession of little-cow-haunted fields, flanked by bits of wall
and bits of hedge, with an amazingly large concentration of redundant (and somewhat
rusting) railway wagons, serving as stores for feeding stuffs. We descended to Ellers,
were Stan was photographed sitting on a Wainwright fence (a short stretch, on open
ground) and eventually began a long descent to Marske.

A welcome awaited us at Marske, a notice directing us to a cottage where cups of tea
were available, the proceeds of selling them being for the local church. Two Coast to
Coasters who had responded to the notice, and were attending to walk-weary feet,
told us of their elaborate two-car scheme; they were now half-way through one of the
stages. The effect was spoiled by the arrival of a taxi, into which they – and their
blistered feet – were transferred to return to base. .

Our path lay through lush fields, by grey scar, veteran yew trees and flower-decked
woodland to Richmond, where our lodgings in Frenchgate were just across the road
from the house wherein lived the 'Sweet Lass of Richmond Hill', made famous by the
song of that name. I had a back room at the lodging place; it offered a splendid view
of the town and the Swale. Bob, appearing from another room in a long white gown,
and with the obligatory camera dangling from his neck, resembled the Ghost of
Richmond Past.

Beyond the town we were in unaccustomed flat country. The wind drew a comb
through miles of sappy grass or expanses of brilliant yellow rape. Hellish experience at
Catterick Bridge, where the Great North Road was full of cars and low-flying lorries.
We thankfully located a riverside path, observed by a dozen mergansers, and headed
out across broad fields, under a big sky. After the torment of the Great North Road,
we entered the peaceful churchyard at Bolton-on-Swale to see the memorial to Henry
Jenkins, who is said to have lived for 169 years. (Untypically, AW had not questioned
the accuracy of the story.)

We followed the meanderings of Bolton Beck. A waterhen jerked and twitched its
way to cover. Two trout, resembling mini-submarines, cruised through sunlit water
near a stone bridge. The Plain of York unfolded under a big sky in which were multi-
storeyed white clouds.  AW had written that the scenery is a hundred per cent rural
and all is tidily arranged.

Our feet were tenderised as we trudged along roads. It was a relief to reach Danby
Wiske and to have an evening meal consisting of beef in Guinness, with mashed
potatoes, carrot and broccoli (all home-grown), followed by apple pie and cream. Luvly!
It was 8th May, 1995, which was VE Day.

At the local inn, mine host rang a bell for two minutes silence.

I glanced through the visitors' book, noticing: "Excellent walk; excellent pub; all Danby Wiske needs now is a chippie, a pizza joint and McDonalds." One Coast to Coaster reported: "Exploding shin; not looking good." Another claimed the only thing missing from the menu was stuffed Wainwright. On the next line, a visitor noted: "Ate that last night." A third entry: "We started off as friends; and now we hate each other!" Overheard: "He's in his third menopause." And: "She goes into Tesco's and the manager appears, waving a white flag."

Beyond Danby Wiske, more big fields. More blotches of yellow rape. More farms with red pantile roofs. And a view along the horizon of the Cleveland Hills. At Ingleby, the menu included a teaser: "Hare, pheasant, venison, lead shot and beater's finger." The visitors' book had the note: "My feet were sore. Now they are dead."

The Coast to Coast zig-zagged through Arncliffe Wood. After moorland walking, we entered Scugdale, where a much-used path was being maintained in top condition. The Coast to Coast enfolded with a crossing of Carlton and Cringle moors. We marvelled at the energy and cash being expensed to reinforce a popular path with stone slabs from Bolton, Lancashire. In view was the Vale of Mowbray and the conical form of Roseberry Topping, locally claimed to be "the highest hill in all Yorkshire."

Coffee was sipped in Lord Stones, which is built into a hillside so as not to upset the planners. On the moors beyond we were greeted by the pilot of a passing hang-glider and had a brief conversation. The Wainstones proved to be a dramatic viewpoint for Bilsdale and the Vale of York.

The highest point of AW's Coast to Coast is Urra Moor, 1,489-ft (455m). The heathery vistas were relieved by standing stones and the now-redundant Ordnance trig point, modern mapping being done from the air. During a long slog on an old railtrack, we followed AW's suggestion – and played trains. Thus we came to the Lion Inn at Blakey, a hostelry dating from 1553.

The roof of the old hostelry came into view as the weather deteriorated. A blizzard hurled flakes of snow horizontally, and in minutes we were in a white-out. When the blizzard petered out, patches of snow remained in the ancient joints of the landscape. Having an evening walk, we found the frost-stiffened grass verges littered with the bodies of countless bumble bees.

Next morning, at 6-10, I glanced from my bedroom window on to a snow-flecked countryside – and watched a ring ouzel, which I have always taken to be both shy and wild, collecting food from among the wooden tables and forms in the hotel grounds. From across the chilled moor came the melancholic double-notes of a golden plover.

We strode from Blakey to Eskdale. It had something of a railway flavour. We paid our respects to Young and Old Ralph and to Fat Betty (moorland crosses), and stood for a while before a memorial to Frank Elgee, who wrote extensively about local topography. The aforementioned ridge walk brought us down into Glaisdale, where the station cafe provided tea and toasted teacake – our favourite snack.

Standing on Beggars Bridge was the thing to do before returning to Wainwright terrain at East Arncliffe Wood, floriferous and full of birdsong. There were flagstones laid down for horse traffic. Egton Bridge brought back memories for me of the annual gooseberry fair and (of course) we negotiated the substantial stepping stones. Ahead was an old toll road – now free of charge – to Grosmont. A steam-hauled train drew into the station on a preserved line. The locomotive was named Eric Treacy.

Our last day on the Coast to Coast began with a climb up a slope approaching that of a house roof. It was a stiff climb from Grosmont to the moors but we eased off while walking down to Littlebeck, where we were mobbed by ducks, and on through a swing-gate marked Falling Foss into sunlit woodland. The path was greasy and puddly after rain. In the woods, a Hermitage cut out from solid rock in 1790 was being used as a picnic place by a school party. Falling Foss, in its woodland setting, roared out like a prophet in the wilderness.

With the sea in sight once again, our pace quickened. There was a quick slog over Greystone Hills, a final tract of moorland before Hawsker, and a path between rows of caravans to the edge of the cliffs, where we came under the gaze of fulmar petrels and herring gulls. At the banktop hotel in Robin Hood's Bay we celebrated our walk with sirloin steak and chips. We ate by candlelight, plus a little moonlight. Another customer at the hotel, requesting steak, said: "I'd like it cooked till it's black and the chef threatens to leave."

We walked into the chilling night air. The moon hung over Baytown like a silver lantern. We pondered on Wainwright and his knack for choosing the most attractive routes between any two places.

*Chapter Eight*

# More about the GBS – With Sue Lawley on a Desert Island – Letters to Bob Swallow – Wainwright at Abbot Hall.

AW was a loner. The only company he tolerated in his fellwandering was his shadow – and, as he observed, that had a habit of disappearing whenever the Weather Clerk drew a curtain of cloud over the fells. We four - Bob, Stan, Colin and myself - went fell-and-dale wandering on alternate Wednesdays. Those walks continued to be our way of escaping from a  mad world to the ageless hills. The Geriatric Blunderers not only endured; they were ritualised.

In a reflective moment, Bob described the GBS as "a unique institution" and, in its outlook and antics, "a cross between Pickwick Papers and Last of the Summer Wine." We sometimes wondered what AW would have thought of us. To him, our membership of four would constitute a crowd.

The first half hour of each walk was invariably spent putting the world to rights. We instituted The Butty Stop. A time for food and drink. Refinement of the basic idea led to the creation of a Major  Butty Stop [between noon and 1 p.m., when a three-course meal was permitted] and two Minor Stops [when the norm was a cup of tea and a biscuit].

The term Butty Stop was attributed by Bob to one Doug Ellis, sometime manager of the Burnley Building Society in Lancaster. Doug was one of those Peter Pan-like characters who never seem to get any older but at the time of which we speak was "pushing eighty". His walking boots were utterly ancient, the toe-ends flapping whenever they got wet. Then they looked for all the world as though they had been borrowed from a circus clown. It was Doug's boast that they had never been cleaned.

His apology for a "cag" was some sort of past wax jacket that had seen previous service on the back of a motor-bike. When not being worn, it stood up by itself. Says Bob: "We owe much to Doug, particularly an inbred ability to get lost at the least provocation."

It was inevitable that with two financial pundits and a surveyor [Stan], the Butty Stop had to have an inbred grading system, 1 to 5. Pluses were added. Minuses were deducted. The finest accommodation at butty-time rated 5+, a status being shared by Stan's living room in Cockermouth after we had been soaked and blown off the fells of Western Lakeland – and a similar spot in Betty Wainwright's home near Kendal. As mentioned, Betty, in a rare moment of recklessness, had accepted the position of Club President. She sometimes wondered what it was all about.

Stan "coined" the word Touroid, a sub-species of tourist governed by an invisible umbilical cord that prevented him or her from straying more than 100 yards from his or her vehicle. Stan was the first to be appointed Duty Foreground, for his attractive and colourful appearance. A somewhat weird aspect of his duties was that of Chief Overtrousers pulleroffer. This alluded to those wretched waterproofs not easily removed over the owner's boots.

Colin used his financial training to good effect when collecting our subs – 50p per person per walk, present or not, the object being to provide our wives with a slap-up feast early in the New Year. Colin organised our annual trip, usually to the Highlands and distilleries of Scotland. His love of photography was put to good use in providing a suitable likeness of the four of us on our annual calendar, a collector's item. Only five calendars were produced. Bob had the onerous problem of compiling statistics and the report on a year's activities and aspirations.

A typical outing of the Geriatric Blunderers, in 1995, was filed in Club records as "Five Wainwrights from Kentmere". On that November day, an easterly wind brought banks of mist to the fells around the head of Kentmere. It also quested for the marrow of our bones. Each sunny spell seemed to last (photographically) for a hundredth of a second before the onset of more mist. Though chilly on the fells, it was quite mild in the dale, especially after over ten miles of hard walking.

Stan met the rest of us at Staveley, near a car notable for an absence of wheels. Bob drove us to the head of Kentmere, a valley we had not seen for some years. Parking was limited. Visitors' cars were already bumper-to-bumper by the church. The expedition began at 9-55 a.m., with a knee-and-ankle-cracking ascent of the Garburn Pass from the head of Kentmere. The Pass had been in such a sad state in 1730 that Benjamin Browne, the magistrate at Troutbeck, ordered it to be repaired; it was "not passable...without danger of being bogged in the moss or lamed among the stones."

On our excursion, the Pass was hardly fit for pedestrians, its stony nature testing our suspension systems. We yearned for another Benjamin Browne. A party of over a hundred chattering fieldfares rose where the landscape was dotted with berried thorn trees. After turning off the Garburn, we walked in acidic country, complete with grey boulders, patterned with lime-green lichen, and expanses of peat bog.

The general tone, from the dead vegetation, was yellow. This being Remembrance

Day, we had two minutes silence. Then we buttyed in the lee of a wall, watching the arrival of a black Labrador that hoovered-up the remains of my Scotch Egg, a delicacy which had in the past proved especially attractive to pheasants.

While dining, we conversed about pronunciation – such as Elger instead of Elgar for the distinguished composer (a fell-walker on visits to Giggleswick, in the limestone country of Yorkshire). We switched to Biblical names, such as Easykyall [Ezekiel]. Bob told of a friend who, when asked to read from Ezekiel in church, could not get her tongue around the prophet's name. Bob rang up the parson, who said she could read a piece from St Matthew instead.

We reached the top of Yoke (2,316-ft) at 11-55 a.m. And discovered that Silurian rock is good cairn-making material. The wind was howling like a Banshee. We moved against it with arched body and bent head – as we had seen in the film Scott of the Antarctic. Staggering, head bent against the wind, and with much sploshing in peat, we reached III Bell at 12-20.

This fell looks like a bell when viewed from the ridge. Two ravens put on an air display. In lyrical mood, I pointed out that the birds were being blown about the blustering sky like charred pieces from a November bonfire. For much of the time we were cocooned in mist, stirred by a lively wind. The route continued upwards, through murk, peat, pools and carpets of sphagnum.

We reached Thornthwaite Crag (2,572-ft) at 1-55. At fourteen feet high, the cairn must be the most imposing in Lakeland. From a distance, it might be confused with a smelt-mill chimney. The lads insisted on me taking a photograph of them, Chad-like, their heads and hands protruding above the capstones of a wall. A watery sun opened its eyes momentarily; then shut them again.

From Thornthwaite Crag, we bestrode a soggy path that, hopefully, would lead us to the summit of Mardale III Bell (2,496-ft). The mist cleared for a moment, during which we looked down towards Hayeswater. As the minutes ticked by, we consulted Mr Wainwright's guide, for Mardale III Bell (unbell-like – just a bluddy great slab of nowt) did not appear to our view.

Stan consulted his compass and demoralised the rest of us by shaking it. (AW had never carried a compass.) We settled down at the head of Nan Bield pass for a repast, glancing downwards on Kentmere Reservoir. The river had been dammed in the 1840s for the paper-making Croppers. It is said that Irish labour was used. Their wild antics caused the magistrates to revoke the licence of the only local inn.

Now we had a four and three-quarter mile plodge back to the car. We waded through half a dozen watercourses, taking extra pains at two becks. The rough track gave way to a rough lane – and the rough lane was succeeded by a green lane, from which we switched course, using stiles and a connecting path. (The little old lanes of Kentmere are a major part of the dale's charm).

By now it was almost dark. We stopped for two or three seconds to admire the misty upper dale, its shades of blue and grey resembling washes on a water-colour painting. Despite a notice "No footpath through churchyard" we traversed the hallowed plot. Our muddy gaiters brushed against some of the graves. We ducked under the branch of a 500-year-old yew tree, sure that we were not violating the spirit of St Cuthbert, patron of the church, for in his day the yew tree, if it existed, would be nobbut a sapling.

Occasionally, we Geriatric Blunderers indulged in fantasy. We organised The Great Cumbrian Bear-Hunt, a concept which surely lay even beyond AW's imaginings. It began at Pooley Bridge. Usually, the day-tripper follows the lakeside road to the head of Ullswater, where mountains appear to leap directly from the water, as in the fjords of Scandinavia. Having had a spell in hospital, I was not capable of tackling one of AW's stern fellside climbs that day.

Bob prescribed an easy walk of five and a half miles. We traversed the low country, looking for bears. AW was fond of animals. He set up a charity to sustain a refuge for dogs. He wrote in a kindly manner about the sheep that were unofficial greenkeepers on the fells. He never mentioned bears.

By chance, I had been reading a newspaper article about a "crusading naturalist's mission to bring back animals from the past." In other words, to let loose on modern society creatures that proved to be something of a pest in history. Brown bears, judging by nature films on television, are not as cuddly and lovable as they looked. And as for wolves...

In preparation for our Lakeland safari, I consulted the Rev H A Macpherson's A Vertebrate Fauna of Lakeland (1892). The worthy clergyman wrote: "I have not detected any historical allusion to the former presence of the Brown Bear in Lakeland." He did mention that remains of this species had been found half-way up the north-west side of Arnside Knott.

Bob led our little party across Pooley Bridge, under the solemn gaze of a wild-looking beast – an Alsatian, which was sitting beside the driver of a small saloon car. The Cumbrian countryside, with its exciting sounds and scents, enveloped us as we quit the bridge-end car park. The Eamont, flowing cool and clear, is a little too lively for the beaver, one of the "animals from the past" mentioned by our new friend, the "crusading naturalist". A fisherman by the weir was seeking brown trout (it being too early for sea trout and salmon).

From high on a bank, where grew a mini-jungle of grasses, came a bedraggled cat, its tail held stiffly upwards in greeting. This surely would have appealed to AW, to whom the cat was a daily companion. This cat adopted us and formed the rearguard. In places, the only evidence it was there came when we saw the end of its tail protruding above the vegetation. At the road, the cat followed the central white line, causing several motorists to stand on their brake pedals.

We regained the fields and looped back to reach the road near Dalemain, the historic home of the Hasell family, who bought it in 1679. This would be good country for auroch, our native wild cattle, which are said to have been extinct 3,200 years ago. Dalemain estate extends from the pastoral landscape near Ullswater to the high fells beyond Martindale, a resort of red deer.

I inquired about bears. Bob switched the subject back to the cat, which we were in the process of losing. Around a cluster of caravans hung the smell of fried bacon. A small boy shouted jubilantly: "Hey – there's a cat!" Sensing that it had a true friend, the cat went to join him. And we tip-toed away. Tip-toeing is not easy if you are wearing boots.

We followed an estate road towards the village of Dacre and lost our jaunty manner when, having advanced on a gate, we found a notice (facing away from us, of course) that warned people to "Beware of the Bull". One of the churchfolk, homeward-bound, doubtless to beef and Yorkshire pudding, after the morning service, confirmed that bears were still to be found at Dacre. He was more specific – there was a bear at each corner of the old churchyard. The thought did not disturb him. There was not so much as a twitch. A shiver ran down my back. It was as though someone had stroked it with an icicle.

In the churchyard at Dacre, we were alarmed by a rustling sound and the sight of a heavy creature bounding away. Our pulses raced, but it was nobbut a sheep. We slipped into Dacre church and bought a copy of a short history of the place. The author, writing about the origin of the village, pronounced it to be very ancient, "as is the name it bears." Bears? Where?

In that lovely old church, we came face to face with strange beasts. A pre-Viking stone on a window ledge had a carving of a winged mustachioed animal, probably a lion. Another carved stone had a panel showing a stag with antlers; a dog-like beast was leaping on to the stag's back. The author of the short history explained: "The hind and hound motif was often used to symbolise the soul pursued by the forces of evil."

Our safari was now extended to take in the churchyard. And, verily, there were bears – four petrified bears, centuries old, smoothed by wind and weather and with a hoary, roughened appearance caused by an encrustation of lichen. It is theorised that the Dacre bears are a humorous rendering of an ancient legend.

One bear slept, its head – or what remains of the head – resting on the top of a pillar. The second bear was turning its head to see what had landed on its back. It was either a cat or a lynx. Bear No 3 was another portrayal of the animal, its right paw flexed over its right shoulder as it tried to dislodge an unwelcome visitor. The fourth bear had a contented appearance. Not only had it caught the aforementioned cat or lynx; it had consumed it!

So we had our bear-hunt – our calm before the rigours of yet another Wainwright fell. The enigmatic Dacre bears now stand in lichened splendour, a puzzle for visitors to consider – and remarkably good scrattin' posts for the local sheep.

AW would have been much amused at the extent to which we took our Blundering. There was an annual get-together, attended by members, their wives – and, usually, foul weather. When Betty was our special guest at a lunch organised at Shap Wells Hotel, around 1,000-ft above sea level, the Weather Clerk laid on a display of snowflakes. In November, 1994, we gathered at an isolated, detached guest house known as The Old Vicarage, Somewhere in Cumbria. (It was actually near Ennerdale Bridge.)

Three days of heavy rain were forecast, with cloud extending across the Atlantic, being particularly dense over our venue. At our chosen haven, Eddie arrived in the lounge with tea before Stan could say "broddle". We repaired to the Fox and Hounds, where I entertained with some scientific experiments, such as a demonstration of the earth's gravitational pull. I allowed my glass of lime-and-lemon to slither off the highly-polished table surface. All but the publican laughed. Someone observed: "The Establishment laughed at Michael Faraday when he said he'd had what he called an electric shock."

Highlight of the evening was the Annual Awards. Best story of the week-end awarded to our hostess, Josie, for her account of a Coast to Coaster's dog belonging to campers. The dog had its own little tent because, as the owner explained, it snored. (As an encore she related the story of a dog belonging to Coast to Coasters. The animal had panniers strapped to its back. These contained – a week's supply of dog food!)

Most Awesome Beard - Blunderer Stan (pending proof that it was Stan behind the beard). Drollest response – A member of the group: "Say something Bob". His reply: "Something Bob." Top of the Blunderers' Pops – "Moon River", selected by Blunderer Colin. (Another entry was rejected. The origin of the sound was in doubt. Music Centre? Or the plumbing system?) Novelty Award – me. I was the first person to walk from Ennerdale Bridge to Ennerdale Water and back again carrying a golf umbrella. Herdwick sheep fair capped [surprised].

Eddie and Josie, our host and hostess, were made honorary members of our club. Eddie wrote: "It felt like being awarded an honorary degree. I can now proudly put the letters Ph.D behind my name – Doctor of Phunosophy!"

In 1985, when sales of his books overtopped the million mark, AW was favourable to personal publicity, through interviews, a television series – and half an hour Radio 4's Desert Island Discs.

The Blunderers were to have a special memory of his island sojourn. We had been trudging in the Eden Valley on an extremely wet day – the sort that, to quote a dale-country saying, looked "as if it'd bin up aw neet."

We left the car beside a village green and arranged to be back there as Sue Lawley announced another instalment of the radio programme in which it is assumed that well-known people will be castaways on a remote island. What would they like to take with them? The windows of the car steamed up. Our sandwiches were soggier than normal.

We smiled at AW's choices of music, especially O what a beautiful Mornin' from the musical Oklahoma. AW referred his questioner to the song's notion that "the sounds of the earth are like music." He preferred that sort of music, instancing the sounds of a mountain stream, twittering birds and a sighing wind on the mountaintops.

There had to be a song about Scotland, so Sue Lawley – or a backroom man – was persuaded to reach for a recording of Kenneth McKellar singing Skye Boat Song. (Which made me think of George Logan, my old Scottish walking friend, who knew Kenneth when he worked for the Forestry Commission and might occasionally be heard making the forest aisles ring with his singing.)

We knew that AW had refused to travel to London for the interview with Sue Lawley and that it was to be broadcast from a Manchester studio. (It reminded me of my own radio debut in that city. The BBC had two rooms in an upper storey of a building overlooking Piccadilly; several of us had been mustered  to express views about rural life; we did so after being taken to a local pub to loosen up our tongues.) On his visit, AW had insisted that afterwards he would be treated to fish and chips.

Listening to the broadcast on a damp day in Edenvale, I scribbled down some of AW's observations. Sue asked him if he was worried at the thought that by becoming best-sellers, the books might destroy some of the old-time peace of the Lake District? AW did not think so. There were more walkers because folk had more money to spend and more leisuretime in which to spend it.

Why had he written about the Lake District in such detail? The guide book project had begun to amuse himself. At Kendal, the fells were handy. Ramblers were not common.  He kept meeting people who were lost. They needed a guide. Writing the guides was also a way of storing up memories for his old age. He might take two things to his desert island. His choice? A photograph of the Blackburn Rovers team that won the FA Cup in 1928 and, of course, a portrait of Betty, the love of his life.

I should have asked AW for his views on the writings of Norman Nicholson, a contemporary, who wrote feelingly about Lakeland fells. Near at hand was Black Combe, which dominated his home territory on the Millom peninsula. Norman was in poor health. I doubt that he ever reached the summit of Black Combe. The Blunderers did so. We saw little because the Weather Clerk had drawn curtains of mist across the scene.

The weather was mild, though a rapid thaw of snow made the ground mushy. Colin, driving from his home near Southport, had a distant view of Black Combe across the bay. Bob, Colin and me met up with Stan in a lay-bye at the western end of the Whitcham Valley. The arrangement was James Bondish, except that Stan, fretful about his car in an area where vandals are not unknown, suggested a tactical retreat to obscure parking spaces within the valley.

Discovering I had left my gaiters behind, I was reconciled to having my boots clogged with snow, for Sod's Second Law decrees that the deepest accumulations of snow are on the footpaths. Bob wore his new anorak, with its startling colour pattern: turquoise, yellow and dark blue. He donned an orange and yellow woolly hat. The nearest sheep panicked.

We entered a mini-valley named Beckside. Beyond, a buzzard rose from beside a small pond and shook its wings in flight, having had no time to drip-dry its plumage. The sheep, concentrated in this low area during a recent blizzard, had spattered the ground with prodigious quantities of droppings/currants/fewmets/crotties. On sloping ground, we zig-zagged, the zigs being long and tolerable; the zags short and sharp. (This situation would have appeal to AW when preparing a diagram.)

Waterproof breeks were donned when we reached our operational elevation of 1,000-ft plus. We floundered in slush and snow, to which was now added the misery of windborne rain and sleet. The cairn on White Combe came into view at 1,361-ft. Here began a weary trek to the cairn and trig column on Black Combe. With thick mist, there was nowt to see.

We ascended to 1,970-ft on a gentle incline rather than having to face a sudden formidable craggy slope. The vegetation was Nardus stricta, which sounds better than the local name – bent. The summit pillar and shelter on Black Combe were viewed when we were almost tripping over them, visibility being down to a few yards. Stan and Bob worked out a compass bearing. We set off with hope that turned to joy when we encountered the main path. Bob's comment of "nae problem" had relief built into it.

On the way down, the mist grudgingly lifted and we had a glimpse of Duddon Estuary and the sea; of shipyard cranes at Barrow and of Walney island, protecting the channel; of snow-streaked fields, groups of windmills and a cluster of caravans at Silecroft. Not

c/o Westmorland Gazette, KENDAL,
14th June 1977

Dear Mr Swallow,

I read your letter with profound dismay.

It is inconceivable that I made an error in quoting the O.S. number on Wild Boar Fell's column. My eyes are not all that good, and the numbers are placed in an awkward place and not always easy to decipher, but I cannot believe that I got my figures wrong.

There are two possibilities to account for the discrepancy you mention. One is that I got on some other summit thinking it was Wild Boar Fell. The second is that you did the same. Neither is even remotely likely. The answer can only be that the number has been changed since my visit.

This opens up the dreadful possibility that the numbers of other trig columns in the district may also have been changed, with dire consequences for me. Therefore I should be extremely glad if you would check the numbers I have quoted when engaged on other expeditions in the area, and report if you find any changes.

I agree about the walk up from Aisgill. But just at present Wild Boar Fell is out of favour with me. But thanks a lot for writing with the sad news.

Yours sincerely,

*AWainwright*

*Letter of June 1977 from AW to Bob Swallow expressing 'profound dismay'.*

classic Wainwright Country but (as they say in Yorkshire) better than nowt.

Bob turned up some letters written by AW and Betty. The oldest, dated June, 1977, was from A Wainwright, his signature being neatly written in his favourite green ink. The letter related to the Ordnance Survey policy of replacing any missing number from a felltop column with the next available number. Until this was resolved, AW could not believe he had made a mistake:

*I read your letter with profound dismay. It is inconceivable that I made an error in quoting the O.S. Number on Wild Boar Fell's column. My eyes are not all that good, and the numbers are placed in an awkward place and not always easy to decipher, but I cannot believe that I got my figures wrong.*

*There are two possibilities to account for the discrepancy you mention. One is that I got on some other summit thinking it was Wild Boar Fell. The second is that you did the same. Neither is even remotely likely. The answer can only be that the number has been changed since my visit.*

*This opens up the dreadful possibility that the numbers of other trig columns in the district may also have been changed, with dire consequences for me. Therefore I should be extremely glad if you would check the numbers I have quoted when engaged on other expeditions in the area, and report if you find any changes.*

*I agree about the walk up from Aisgill. But just at present Wild Boar Fell is out of favour with me. But thanks a lot for writing with the sad news.*

In April of the following year, AW was contrite:

*Thank you for your further letter about the mystery of Wild Boar Fell.*

*I no longer have doubts as to the veracity of your statements regarding the O.S. Number on their column. I have no doubts either that the number was 10797 when I was there in 1971. I have been able to find the 6" map I used on that occasion and my pencil note, made on the site, is quite clear.*

*It does seem, therefore, that the number has been altered in recent years. I do occasionally have contact with the O.S. local office, and next time will confirm the change and let you know the explanation.*

*Thanks for writing.*

Bob, writing to AW, in March, 1979, proposed that a panoramic view of the Lakeland fells to be seen from Morecambe promenade would be an attractive feature. AW replied:

*Thank you for your letter and interesting proposition.*

*I can't recall that I have ever clearly seen the Lakeland skyline from Morecambe and I would think the distance too great to make an effective panorama, the summits being too closely bunched to be easily distinguished.*

*However, if you keep your camera in readiness in the office, and nip out to the sands when you get an hour of exceptional clarity, preferably using a telephoto lens, and can produce black and white blowups that show the skyline sharply, then, if you wish, I will have a shot at drawing the view.*

*I doubt whether such a panorama would be a commercial success. There can be few days in any year when conditions are absolutely right and inspire interest, and, further, most visitors to Morecambe are more interested in indentifying the more intimate local attractions such as ice-cream stalls and bathing belles. Most of them, poor souls, have not learned to raise their eyes to the hills.*

*It's a nice idea, though, and I pass it back to you for further action if you want to go on with it.*

From A Wainwright (green ink) to Mr Swallow, November, 1979:

*There has been a sequel to our correspondence about the number of the Ordnance column on Wild Boar Fell.*

*A few weeks ago I had a letter from a walker who told me that I had made a mistake in the chapter on Black Combe (in 'The Outlying Fells') where I quoted the Ordnance column number as 2953. The number, he reported, was 11602. I was confident that I had not been in error, and told him so.*

*Unknown to me, he then wrote to the Ordnance Survey to settle the matter, and has just sent me their reply, from which I learn that all their columns are inspected every ten years and repaired if necessary. Latterly they have been finding many vandalised and the number plates stolen, no doubt as mementos. Their records show that an inspection of the one of Black Combe in July 1976 showed that a complete rebuilding was needed and this was done. As the former number plate 2953 could not be found, a new one with the number 11602 was affixed.*

*The same thing must have happened on Wild Boar Fell – we were both right!*

From A Wainwright (blue ink) to Mr Swallow, October, 1980:

*Thank you for sending me a copy of your staff magazine which is really very nicely produced and printed.*

*The highspot of its contents was of course the gripping account by Fellsman of some of his more nail-biting exploits on the fells. This was good reading indeed and I enjoyed it thoroughly. (Three mis-spellings of names must be faults of the printer.)*

*I look forward eagerly to Part Two of the saga, and hope I may be similarly privileged to receive a copy.*

From A Wainwright to Mr Swallow, 1st June, 1981:

*Thank you for your very kind invitation of 14th May. I regret the delay in replying but received your letter only an hour ago on my return from a holiday in Snowdonia.*

*I am very conscious that you do me an honour, and it pains me to decline. Public speaking has never been my forte and now that I am old and, according to my friends, rapidly becoming senile, the occasion would be too much of an ordeal for me – and certainly for my audience. I am sorry, but happily for all concerned I know my limitations.*

*Sorry again. It was nice of you to invite me. I hope the evening is a success.*

Bob was manager of the new Lancaster branch of the Leeds Permanent Building Society; in October, 1982, he informed AW about it. And mentioned his son's ascent of Jack's Rake. AW replies:

*The continuing saga of the Ordnance Survey column on Wild Boar Fell.*

c/o Westmorland Gazette,
KENDAL, Cumbria,

19th November 1979

Dear Mr Swallow,

There has been a sequel to our correspondence about the number of the Ordnance column on Wild Boar Fell.

A few weeks ago I had a letter from a walker who told me that I had made a mistake in the chapter on Black Combe (in 'The Outlying Fells') where I quoted the Ordnance column number as 2953. The number, he reported, was 11602. I was confident that I had not been in error, and told him so.

Unknown to me he then wrote to the Ordnance Survey to settle the matter, and has just sent me their reply, from which I learn that all their columns are inspected every ten years and repaired if necessary. Latterly they have been finding many vandalised and the number plates stolen, no doubt as mementos. Their records show that an inspection of the one on Black Combe in July 1976 showed that a complete rebuilding was needed and this was done. As the former number plate 2953 could not be found, a new one with the number 11602 was affixed.

The same thing must have happened on Wild Boar Fell -- we were both right!

Yours sincerely,

awainwright

38 Kendal Green, KENDAL, Cumbria, LA9 5PP

Election Day

Dear Mr Swallow,

    I am sorry to have taken so long in applying myself to your project of a view from Morecambe Bay.  Absence from home on holiday is the reason for the delay.

    I now have your photographs, and I must say that they are not as good as I hoped.  My failing eyesight can barely discern the mountain background, and in places not at all, and I could not possibly work from your pictures.  The middle distances (on the north side of the Bay) are clear enough, and I think therefore prepare first of all a drawing of the low country across the Bay and then go to the jetty, with binoculars, and superimpose the mountain skyline.  In this way I should be able to complete the job at home.  Of course I must choose a day of perfect visibility for my vigil on the jetty, and since such days are rare, some further delay is inevitable.

    I will submit the drawing in due course, but it may mean a wait of months before I can do so,  Please be patient a little longer.

Yours sincerely,
A Wainwright

*'Election Day' communication from AW asking the recipient to be 'patient a little longer'.*

*I am pleased to learn that the opening of the Lancaster branch [of the Leeds Permanent Building Society] was so successful. I hope it continues to prosper. I have considered your kind suggestion about the sale of Christmas cards. Whilst we want to sell as many as we can, I really don't think you should be put to the trouble of collecting and accounting for them. So Jack's Rake has succumbed to a 12-year-old. I always thought it was a route for tough he-men only! My congratulations.*

From A Wainwright: simply headed Election Day:

*I am sorry to have taken so long in applying myself to your project of a view from Morecambe Bay. Absence from home on holiday is the reason for the delay. I now have your photographs and I must say they are not a good as I hope. My failing eyesight can barely discern the mountain background and in places not at all.*

*I could not possibly work from your pictures and I must therefore prepare first of all a drawing of the low country across the Bay and then go to the jetty, with binoculars, and superinpose the mountain skyline. Of course, I must choose a day of perfect visibility for my vigil on the jetty. Since such days are rare, some further delay is inevitable.*

*I will submit the drawing in due course, but it may mean a wait of months before I can do so. Please be patient a little longer.*

*[Bob: Remarks over my photography were not shared by Betty, who promptly took AW to an optician. Diagnosis – his sight was failing.]*

AW writes to Bob in May, 1985. He uses green ink:

*Thank you for your letter, copy of magazine and photos. You are certainly doing Michael [Bob's son] proud – I note he appears in this month's Cumbria, too. Good lad! Well done. The memorial photo is excellent and I am glad to know it is surviving the years.*

*The one of the shelter on Great Borne does not revive any recollections: I must have missed it. Remarkable to find it is so unfrequented a spot: I think it must have been erected by the local shepherd for his own use. Don't mention Black Hill to me! I hope your campaign for loans (and new prints) is doing well enough to justify your optimism.*

AW, writing in June, 1986, refers to a recent BBC TV series of Walks with Wainwright:

*Thank you so much for a very kind letter (one of over a hundred received these past few weeks). The TV series seems to have been well received according to BBC's "audience research" and they have now asked me to do a similar series on Scotland for 1987. Bill would enjoy your Skiddaw itinerary – a favourite area of mine. I will get in touch with Bill when things have settled down. Thank you for your offer of further help with your super new equipment, which I will bear in mind.*

38 Kendal Green, Kendal
1st May 1985

Dear Bob,

Thankyou for your letter,
copy of magazine and photos.
You are certainly doing Michael
proud — I note he features
in this month's 'Cumbria' too.
Good lad! well done.

The Gill memorial photo is
excellent, and I am glad to
know it is surviving the
years. The one of the shelter
on Great Borne does not revive
any recollections: I must have
missed it. Remarkable to
find it in so unfrequented a
spot: I think it must have
been erected by the local
shepherd for his own use.

Don't mention Black Hill to me!

I hope your campaign for
loans (and new prints) is doing
well enough to justify your
optimism.

Yours sincerely
AWainwright.

*An original letter in the famous green ink.*

*Betty Wainwright and Bill Mitchell, on a green lane above Dentdale.*

From AW – November, 1987:

*Thank you for your letter and its exciting news of the super audio-visual equipment you have acquired. We paid a visit to Bill Mitchell the other week on the eve of his retirement. Betty would be delighted to tag along with you, or you and Bill, when you next have a none-too-strenuous valley walk planned.*

From Betty to her friends – 1991:

*Thank you for the kind wishes you have expressed following AW's death. It has been a great comfort to me at this sad time to know my husband was held in such affectionate regard by so many people. Personal footnote to Bob: I am so grateful for your kind letter. I'll be in touch before long.*

From Betty to Bob – June, 1991:

*I think I have sold the house and complete for the bungalow in Burneside at the end of next month so should be moving at the beginning of August. After that, life should be simpler and I should have more free time. I'll have to get in trim again before daring to suggest I go with you and Bill. My knees are not as supple as they should be! Keep in touch.*

From Betty – March, 1995:

*I have been tidying my desk and came across these slides, which must date from a request from AW for a picture of the service on Great Gable (I think!). I am so sorry they have not been returned before – and hope you haven't been looking for them for some other purpose.*

From Betty – September, 1997:

*Thank you very much for the latest account from the BWC [Betty's reference to Blunderers' Walking Club]. I really enjoy reading these reports – they bring back so many memories of days on the fells with AW. Wonderful! I was particularly interested in this latest one because my very first outing with him was to this area.*

*It was the 30th of October, 1962. He had been in correspondence with a Mrs Lewis (an avid fan) and because at that time she was elderly and ill he wanted to visit her. She lived in a cottage called Badger Hill at Nether Row. We called on her and she was delighted and told us that during the war she was asked by the Civil Service in London, for whom she worked, if she would be evacuated to the Carlisle area along with other civil servants. When told violets and primroses grew in the hedgerows, she agreed.*

*She came along with her son. She said he had died in the previous year and she'd had a seat placed on High Pike in his memory. They both loved the area and she never thought of returning south (who can blame her?). She did not tell us the nature of his death – nor was her husband mentioned. I am glad there is a similar memorial to her.*

*Top of the world: a Wainwright enthusiast breaks the skyline on Glaramara.*

*I am now going to the Kendal midday concert – the first of the season – and afterwards to buy a new folder for our walking club reports.*

Letters that I received from AW in the 1980s revealed the gentle side of his nature. On 15 September, 1984, he mentioned a manuscript he had been given to read. The author was a teacher who had lived near Kendal for many years. AW wrote that his manuscript, titled The North Road, dealt with the history of the old road between Kendal and Shap "with a descriptive account of the route (which can still be seen and followed for most of the way) and is supplemented by a portfolio of his own black and white photographs."

The author had asked AW to write to me on his behalf by way of introduction. He let him down gently. "You would find his manuscript interesting but I fear not a viable proposition because of its lack of general appeal. I have expressed this opinion to him, but it would give him a measure of satisfaction if only he could see a real live Editor with it. He is prepared for disappointment. I hope you will grant him the favour of an interview."

I was producing lots of paperbacks, mostly under the Castleberg imprint. Some of these were given to AW. In the month of Christmas, 1988, he wrote: "So many good things are coming out of Giggleswick these days that it is not easy keeping in step. I must thank you for the Elgar leaflet and now for your splendid Changing Dales, a book [published by Dalesman] that has been crying out to be written for a long time, a story you have told and illustrated with a wonderful selection of pictures.

"Your proposal to write a similar volume for Cumbria is excellent news. Betty is having a hectic time at present in the continuing absence of a Warden [for the animal centre] but will be delighted to attempt a foreword when you are in a position to produce a few specimen pages. [Which she did.] AW added: "Relax over Christmas. You are supposed to be retired, remember. Sincerely, AW."

I sent AW material relating to my proposed book entitled It's a Long Way to Muckle Flugga. He looked through "your Scottish narrative" with interest – and, as mentioned in chapter 6, some misgivings. A friend had provide a sketch map, which AW denounced as "awful". He could not understand my selection of place-names nor the locations I had given them - "Crianlarich in the North Sea, the Caledonian Canal apparently issuing at Aberdeen. There is no clue as to the black patches and the sprinkling of dots and no scale of miles. It is dreadful, badly drawn, misleading and unintelligible. You must omit it or substitute a much better one."

AW was nonetheless honoured by my invitation to write a foreword – "providing you cut out the map and any others you may think of including – and correct some of the place names in the narrative, which is otherwise interesting and especially good on the natural life of the northern districts." AW added a postscript: "As an alternative title, what about It's a Long Way to Cape Wrath, which everbody has heard about?"

He wrote the foreword, as promised, and in the accompanying letter, dated 22 July, 1988, apologised for holding on to the manuscript for so long. "I was unable to read it myself and had to depend on Betty to find time in her hectic life to make me familiar with its contents. I found it entertaining and enjoyable, and it revived many memories of happy days spent in the places you describe so well."

In May of the following year, I received two letters from Betty. I had sent AW and Betty a copy of my latest Yorkshire book. "I took it with us when we went to Goathland last week. (We were there filming the last stage of the Coast to Coast Walk.) It was very appropriate reading. It is next on the list of my 'to be read aloud to AW books!'" In the second letter, Betty hoped I would have an interesting visit to St Kilda. "We'll be thinking of you – look forward to another walk on your return. All the best from both of us."

A letter – scribbled, in pencil – reached me in February, 1992. Betty wished me good luck with my latest book "and thank you for the dedication and all your nice comments about my beloved lad. Do come to Burneside this spring. Sincerely. Betty."

AW had retired as Borough Treasurer in 1967. In 47 years of local government work, he had not missed a day through illness. When he left his office at the Town Hall, it was a clean break – he would not return. He did not propose to give up work on his drawings – or his connections with voluntary organisations. Especially the charity known as Animal Rescue Cumbria, which, with other worthy causes, had absorbed the profits from his books - in all, some half a million pounds.

His 80th birthday gave Vicky Slowe, Director of Abbot Hall at Kendal, and her staff, a chance to thank him for his labours on behalf of the Gallery and Museums. An exhibition was organised; it confirmed that this quiet, shy, caring man had given much time to worthy causes. AW was on the steering committee that established the Lake District Art Gallery and Museum Trust. He was, indeed, the Trust's first honorary treasurer. AW handled the finances of the (then) Kendal Borough Museum and was its honorary Clerk.

On view at Abbot Hall were original drawings from his books, examples of his penmanship in Town Hall accounts from many years back – and the local Water Board accounts, which became known as "the illustrated annual accounts". Training at Blackburn Town Hall had given AW a love of words and figures; their use became an art.

A photograph of local government employees at Kendal Town Hall included a middle-age AW, centre, and on his left Percy Duff, who became his successor as Borough Treasurer. We saw drawings that predated the guides, his pens and also a distinctive

A pair of well-used Wainwright boots in a Kendal exhibition.

Wainwright pipe, which had a special alloy stem. A pair of his fellwandering boots, on loan from Bookworm of Kendal, were old-fashioned, inexpensive and undoubtedly well-worn. Some padding around the ankles offered the walker extra protection on rocky upland paths.

The sight of those old, worn boots remained with me. I was thinking of them one March day when in the company of three other walking friends - Roy, Cyril and Terry - I undertook a nine and a-half mile walk on the fells, taking in the summits of Place Fell, Angle Tarn Pikes and Satura Crags, which Wainwright had recommended as a splendid viewpoint for Bannerdale.

The weather was a typical Lakeland concoction at the beginning of spring: misty, then mizzly, becoming drizzly, then rainy – with a dash of hail! We were soon motoring over Kirkstone Pass to Hartsop and the joys of a free car park within sight of a majestic assembly of fells. We strode through the village, four-abreast, and I pointed out a bungalow perched on rocks. The owner, a Lancashire lady, had a rock garden in a literal sense. She had to tend those plants growing from rocks by dangling at the end of a rope.

We passed the entry to a drive leading to a mohair farmshop without sighting a "mo". Catkins hanging from a hazel shook like lambs' tails in a gentle breeze. We were in a Lakeland of mossy walls, mossy trees and mossy boulders. Our way led to a track crossing Angle Beck below a series of cascades which, in their dominant whiteness, resembled illustrations from Wainwright guides.

Our track tilted skywards. Roy said: "The honeymoon is over." Terry remarked: "Back to work." We plodded upwards, in bottom gear. The valley had the misted appearance of an old-fashioned kitchen on wash-day. On the sloping ground, gnarled thorns grew from inhospitable screes. With greater height, we saw a good deal of Patterdale. Brotherswater was now in view. Farm dogs were passing the morning sending barked messages to each other.

At Stonebarrow Gill there were more gnarled thorns. At the top of the Hause, drizzle became steady rain, beating a tattoo on our anorak hoods. We attained the summit of Place Fell (1,254-ft), Roy announced he had now climbed 219 summits at over 2,000-ft. It included two previously unvisited Wainwrights. As we began a steep descent, a raven glided by. The bird had forgotten to raise its undercarriage. Or was it using its dangling legs to stabilise it in gusty conditions?

Lunch was taken at the Boredale Hilton, which was Roy's name for what remained of an old-time sheep croft. A skylark sang, not very well. Was it rehearsing? A meadow pipit descended in "shuttlecock flight", its wings and tail held stiffly upwards as it fell. The bird was uttering a warbly song. On attaining Angle Tarn Pike (north), we were saluted by a passing raven. A peaty path led us to Angle Tarn Pike (south), which was one metre lower than its twin.

AW had mentioned the not-often-visited Satura Crag as a splendid viewpoint for Bannerdale. Roy bounded up the slope like a mountain goat, with the rest of the party moving somewhat less goat-like behind him. The view that opened out included a glimpse of The Nab, Martindale and the best land, vivid green now it was early spring. Also in clear view was Bannerdale, complete with clusters of trees and an assembly of red deer, too far away to be observed in detail.

Dark clouds massed in the north-west. The first hailstones bounced off our anorak hoods. We descended towards Hartsop in a wind that howled like part of the sound track to a Bronte film. Hailstones pattering on our waterproofs might have been part of nature's percussion section. The shower cleaned the atmosphere. On the final descent to Hartsop, we saw everything with clarity and colour. There were three hearty cheers – for Mr Wainwright.

 We returned to the same area in April to bag five 2,000-footers and three Wainwrights in a high fell sortie calculated at eight and a-half miles; it seemed like ten. As we left the car in a park near the outflow of Brotherswater, we saw great fells banded by golden light. There was beauty close at hand. The ground was spangled by flowers – by celandine, primrose, violet and wood anemone.

Roy kept up a lively pace; he was, in the parlance of Lakeland fox-hunters, a "straight-necked 'un." A stile we used as we headed for Hoggill Brow was of the step variety. Large pieces of slate extended through the wall, providing steps on either side. AW would undoubtedly have noticed that the top step had three holes, proclaiming it was once a gate-stoop.

We climbed towards Hartsop Above How (1,870-ft). Gavel Pike, a steeple-like fell, came into view. We walked over sodden ground where black slugs luxuriated. Claiming our attention, beyond Deepdale, was mighty Fairfield. As we rested on a grassy knoll, Cyril provided coffee and Terry produced some of his wife's splendid Victoria sponge cake. Our knoll seemed to be the summit of Hartsop Above How but, according to Wainwright, was not. The true summit lay 200 yards away to the north-east.

The wall that had been our guide to the upper fell country took another course. We were left looking at two fells that would be the next to fall to us. There was Hart Crag (2,698-ft) and Dove Crag (2,603-ft). We were now on a grassy ridge, with peaty soft spots, between Dovedale and Deepdale, each valley being far below us. Roy looked at his map. We waited, anxiously, for his verdict. Happily, he does not resort to shaking the map and looks pleased. We plod on.

As the climb steepened, we re-shaped a scree slope and then mounted on grass-lined steps sufficiently large for a giant. The path levelled out near the ruckle of boulders on which was the cairn marking the summit of Hart Crag. It was occupied by a party of German visitors. We did not see any bath towels which, at coastal resorts, are used territorially. On Fairfield Horseshoe, we settled down to eat at a spot sheltered from the gaze of other walkers. Subsequently, we bagged summits in quick succession - Dove Crag, Black Brow (2,100-ft), thence across Nardus stricta ground to an obscure hump called Scandal Head (2,050-ft), from which we saw Scandale, extending westwards, dipping towards Ambleside.

Roy led us to Little Hart Crag (2,091-ft), where we were joined by a young couple, members of the Hash House Harriers, founded in Kuala Lumpur in 1938 and – like the Wainwright Society – having members across the world. On to High Hartsop Dodd, where the path dipped steeply. As we completed the walk beside Brotherswater, we heard the attractive ditty of a willow warbler – and the raucous voice of a visitor calling to his young. We had, that day, climbed a total of 3,100-ft.

*Chapter Nine*

# Walking with Betty – Joss Naylor's Astonishing Run – A Wainwright Society – Derry Brabbs – Crampons on Wetherlam.

When Wainwright retired in December, 1990, there was a discussion at The Westmorland Gazette on what he might be presented with to mark almost 30 years as his publishers. Andrew Nichol, book publishing manager, made a direct approach to AW – what would he like? The answer was surprising (perhaps not, to those who knew him). AW requested four Cornetto ice creams, which were purchased at a local corner shop. Betty handed one of the Cornetto's to him and a second one was offered to Andrew. AW shook his head. All of them had been intended for him; the remaining three should be kept in the refrigerator.

AW's fell-walking days were over. Bob and Betty, with AW's blessing, had occasional forays on the hills. I was invited to make up a threesome. One dry but cloudy afternoon, we left AW sitting (and smoking) in the car, in a corner of the popular parking zone at Dent Town. AW, slumped in his seat, hoped to remain inconspicuous. Our path led up Flintergill, around the Green Lane to the head of Deepdale, and back to Dent by that quiet, delectable valley.

Into view came a local farmer, who had just clambered from his tractor. He was wearing wellies - one green, one black. I commented that this was odd. Said the farmer: "Nay – at home, I've got another pair of wellies just like 'em." On our return to the car park, we found a fretful AW, who had left the car only once – to visit the toilet. On the way, someone had had recognised and accosted him. He was not pleased.

Anyone who had seen the lonesome AW on the fells had a conversation-stopping recollection. Norman Wordsworth and his wife, keen fell-walkers, were trudging along one of the higher sections of the Nidderdale Way when they saw a lone walker some distance behind them. "When we stopped for our morning coffee, he caught up with us and said: "If he hadn't been dead, I would have thought you were Wainwright!" Norman could not resist saying: "No, I am not Wainwright. I am Wordsworth!"

*Joss Naylor (right) with his wife and old friend in Wasdale.*

When, in later years, AW was still zig-zagging but mainly on level ground, he featured in a series of BBC films. An admirer of Wainwright, his prose and his draughtsmanship, was surprised by his observation, in the Pennine Way, that "nobody loves Bleaklow". He begged to differ from AW, stating: "Most dedicated walkers that I know consider the hill unique and the traverse over the highest route from the Flouch to Ladybower is one of the best walks in the Peak.

"On reaching Pinaw Beacon, he quite rightly admires the view northward and looks forward to the delights of the limestone Dales. It seems surprising that the view north-west to the eastern Lakeland Fells is not mentioned. I think this must be the first point on the Pennine Way from which the Lakes can be seen."

At Wasdale Show, in 1987, I had a brief chat with a man whose athletic achievement associated with the Wainwrights is unlikely to be beaten. I refer to Joss Naylor who, in July, the previous year, completed the Wainwright Round of 391 miles, and a total climb of 121,000-ft, in 7 days, 1 hour and 25 minutes. Whew! I asked Joss how he organised his walk. His reply was: "I did a book a day!"

Hot weather had characterised the first five days. Joss could think of little else but ice cream. There followed a spell of wind and rain. The book-a-day notion was first developed by Chris Bland, an athletic stonemason, who had the grand idea of linking the Wainwright peaks, though in his scheme 22 of the peaks were omitted. His run was sponsored; the money raised went towards repairing the roof of Borrowdale church.

Joss, who farmed near the head of Wasdale, was in his 50th year when he undertook the run for charity, this being the Arthritis and Rheumatism Council, which had just celebrated its half century. On his run, which was co-ordinated by Ken Ledward, Joss had a goodly number of pacers and helpers. On July 4, he ascended Castle Crag in Borrowdale, which was followed by his final summit, Barrow, a jog into Keswick and a greeting from Gillian, his daughter. He had worn out three pairs of fell shoes.

Before I retired from the editorship of Cumbria in 1988, I had the awesome experience when "putting the magazine to bed" of passing between white cliffs formed of paper earmarked for the ever-chattering printing press that was kept solely for Wainwright books. During my time with the magazine, a million copies of Wainwright books were published; they absorbed 200 tons of paper.

Book sales eventually exceeded two million.

I was invited to the inaugural meeting of the Wainwright Society, held at Ambleside Youth Hostel on a November day in 2002. Someone wrote: "I'd like to think that Wainwright would be amused by the setting up of this society, but somehow I don't think he would have come to the meeting." It was packed. AW was allergic to crowds. So, I presume, were most of the people present. They were there out of regard for

Wainwright.

Earlier, I had tried to find a few square feet of parking space in the hostel grounds. There was not even space for a scooter. Moving between rows of cars and mini-buses were young people geared up for fell-walking or water-skiing. AW would have shuddered, then slunk away from the motley throng. Eventually, I brought the car to rest in a public park (£1.80 for four hours.) Cafes were closed. A wishing-well was clogged by dead leaves.

At the hostel, I followed signs to "Wainwright AGM". I chatted with Terry Fletcher, editor of Cumbria and himself a keen fellsman. There was time to exchange greetings with Eric Robson, who had accompanied AW on his television rounds of Lakeland and Scotland. (I had last met Eric when he interviewed me at Ribblehead viaduct and at Clapham for items in a series of walks transmitted by Border Television.)

In the main room of the Youth Hostel on Wainwright Day were fans from the far corners of the land, also representatives of the Tourist Board. The room had seating for precisely fifty people. Eric, dark-haired, brisk, with a deep mike-trained voice well-known to listeners to Gardeners' Question Time on BBC Radio was affability itself. He proved to be the ideal chairman (and was, indeed, elected to this position). Eric has a fund of amusing tales, including one of a Lakeland farmer who objected to AW, in a guide, directing people across three of his fields "to a green gate". The farmer subsequently had the gate painted black.

Item six on the agenda was "Do we want to form a Wainwright Society?" Eric presumed from the attendance that the answer was yes. "What will be the aims of this Society?" Many and varied, from publishing a journal to arranging walks. (AW, of course, liked to walk alone.) At an election of officers, Betty, who could not be present because of ill-health, was accorded the distinction of becoming Life President. Many of those attending, wearing outdoor togs and holding well-worn rucksacks, climbed Dove Crag, high on Fairfield Horseshoe, which was being trumpeted as the first peak climbed by AW, fifty years ago to the day. Was it really the first peak? AW would presumed have crossed one or two others to reach it. And, of course, there had been Orrest Head, where in 1930 AW's conversion to Lakelandism took place.

That day, I felt the spirit of the man would be detectable on Orrest Head, the modest sub-800-ft eminence above Windermere. And that is where I went, having been refuelled with egg sandwiches and coffee at Booths supermarket in Windermere. I shared the hill with a man holding the hand of a toddler, a couple who were "admiring the view" and a middle-aged lady who, spurning the tarmac way, had made a scratchy bee-line through autumn-tinted woodland.

AW and his cousin, on that first visit, seventy-two years before, had emerged from woodland and, as though a curtain had been dramatically torn aside, beheld a magnificent view. "It was a moment of magic, a revelation so unexpected that I stood transfixed, unable to believe my eyes." Excitedly, I picked out Scafell Pike among the blue-grey humps on the horizon. To the south-west gleamed Morecambe Bay.

Wainwright had been by no means the first Lancashireman to cut loose from the gritty background of mills, pubs, chapels and terrace housing to settle in the Lake District. His inclinations were similar to those of Joseph Hardman, who quit milldom for Kendal and for many years – as a full-time photographer of note – joyously explored the Lake District, leaving the area once a year – to have a week's holiday at Blackpool.

Joseph had a plate camera and a hefty tripod which was put in place by his wife. He travelled to his chosen areas by taxi, sometimes with pretty nurses from the Kendal hospital. They were posed in the foreground of some of his Lakeland views, being guaranteed to attract picture editors on newspapers and magazines.

Photography was to come prominently into the Wainwright story – and not just the many thousands he took to be artistically copied in his line illustrations. As Editor of Cumbria, backing up articles with photographs, I was familiar with the work of Derry Brabbs, who had provided the colour photographs for a series of books written by Wainwright.

In 1991, I interviewed Derry for Cumbria magazine. He was not boastful. He told me that as a child, he often had a box Brownie camera in his hand. His entry into landscape photography came after three years of study at Leicester Art College. He then undertook commercial work, including advertising in London. He moved back to Yorkshire in 1973.

I first met Derry over ten years before at a literary event in Leeds. It was the launch of James Herriot's Yorkshire, the photographic commission for which kept Derry busy for over a year. As Herriot wrote the manuscript, Derry went out and illustrated it. Derry, a Yorkshireman (born in Sheffield, 1947) had provided the many stunning colour photographs of fell and moor, dale and sea cliff for the best-selling Herriot book.

After Herriot came illustrative work for two companion books, one relating to Wales (Wynford Vaughan Thomas) and the other to the West Country (Angela Rippon). There was also work on a book about the Thames. "I then wrote to Michael Joseph, the publisher, saying that no one had done a decent book on the Pennine Way and that it was coming up to the 20th anniversary of the official opening of this long distance footpath that crossed some of the most glorious scenery in England. It seemed a shame that no work existed that had been illustrated in colour." He added that the only books available about the Pennine Way were little pocket guides such as the ones devised by Wainwright.

Victor Morrison, managing director of Michael Joseph, was a keen walker who knew

*Derry Brabbs, whose photography has featured in the Wainwright books.*

of Wainwright's books. He recommended to the senior editor that AW should be invited to write a book. He agreed. After Fellwalking came Pennine Way and Coast to Coast Walk. Both were photographed in good conditions, though Derry made the traditional error on Kinder Scout. He got lost among the peat bogs. "I think everyone has done that."

He got on well with Wainwright. Mountain photography was taken up almost by accident; he was "not too good" on heights, which was "bad news for someone who is supposed to hang off the edges of cliffs by his finger-tips." His collaboration with AW began with Fellwalking with Wainwright, published in 1984. He illustrated eighteen of the author's favourite walks in Lakeland. "Until I got teamed up with AW, I had not done any serious walking. So it is entirely due to him that I have been punished this way..."

AW was in the habit of doing his own page layouts, typing out the manuscripts and leaving spaces for photographs. "It has made life very easy." The difficult bit was securing photographs of sufficiently high quality in a region where the mountains do not always have sunlight upon them.

"Light is the be-all-and-end-all," said Derry. "Look at any stone wall or rock that has a piece of sunlight on it, and then look at one that has no sunlight on it, and you will see that one piece of rock is alive and the other is dead.

"It is the same with mountains. If you photograph in sunshine, it means that the rocks show their true colours and textures and all the cracks and crevices are well defined. If you are photographing without sunshine on a relatively dull day, then all those details are lost. Success also relates to being in the right place at the right time – knowing, for instance, that if you want to photograph Bowfell Buttress it has got to be done in the morning because that is the only time it will have strong light on it."

This was not easy for Derry, who lives at the village of Nidd, near Harrogate some 75 miles from the heart of Lakeland. All Derry's photography is done on 35mm film and he is sparing in the use of colour filters. He does like to fit a graduated grey filter to his camera to bring the sky into parity with the foreground. "Skies to me, especially in the Lakes, are an integral part of the pictures."

He is unhappy on steep scree. One winter day, when he was photographing Bowfell Buttress, he went along the Climbers' Traverse to where there is a huge scree run, which this day was covered with snow. "I was walking across it when it started moving. I was unsure what to do – to go forward or go back. Meanwhile, the boulders were grinding and rolling underfoot." He was right for about ten minutes, then told himself he would not achieve anything just standing there. He went forward, clear of danger.

Derry marvels at what AW has achieved in his lifetime. "Every time I look at his books and his drawings and consider that one man has done all this, and more, I feel bone idle and humble." He does not often camp on the hills. "I have just too much tackle to carry, without the help of Sherpas." He favours a good camp site, such as that provided by the National Trust at the head of Langdale. "The site is right on the end of Mickleden."

When I met him, he had spent two days camping in Langdale, waiting for a chance to go up Bowfell and carry on with some work on another Wainwright book about Lakeland. "Yesterday was a complete wash-out and today I went hunting for an ancient sheepfold that AW had written about. It is a secluded fold not visible from the floor of the dale and reputedly used for stock when the Scots were raiding. I got about three photographs of it. Three photographs for two days' work: this is not good!" He is all for blue skies and fluffy white clouds – for Utopian England. "One has to have the clarity. If you cannot see the definition on the landscape, taking pictures is a waste of time."

Mention any Lakeland peak and the memories spill out. "Wasdale Head has to be the mecca of places; you get that glorious view about three-quarters of a mile before you get to the end of the lake, with Pillar, Scafell and Great Gable all gradually coming into sight." At Nidd, there was family life, with a wife and two daughters. Like the bee, he counts the sunny hours. As our conversation ended, I was not to know that before the words could be printed AW, a good friend of us both, would have died and his ashes would have been scattered on Haystacks.

When I met John Bulman, a Langdale man who grew up in the 1930s, I became aware of the upsurge of interest in Lakeland fells that was ultimately met by AW's guides. In the 30s, John had seen few walkers and cyclists. Motor cycle trials were held on the high passes. "We didn't think of the likely consequences. We all laughed when Robert Spence drew Buttermere with a funicular on the fellside and pictured double-decker buses going over Honister Pass."

After the Second World War, the number of visitors had risen dramatically, to the detriment of the landscape. There was "wild" camping, tents being pitched wherever people felt inclined. In the 1960s, an influx of working-class climbers occurred. The men were brave, competent and in such numbers they buzzed like flies round every suitable crag.. "They had a lot of tackle," said John. "When I saw them coming down from the fell with their pitons, their nuts and bolts and spanners clanking, I was reminded of shire horses at an agricultural show. Climbing was an absolute craze at that time."

When Bob and I ticked off Wetherlam in winter, I was introduced to ice-axe and crampons. Only Bob had the crampons. Being volcanic in origin, I half expected to find Wetherlam, one of the Coniston giants, still warm after its fiery baptism. At the time of our visit it was plated with ice. The lowering clouds deposited hailstones, not rain.

I thought of AW's advice to me, when I met him at his home. He wished me good walking – "and don't forget – watch where you are putting your feet." When I had mentioned to AW the 2,502-ft Wetherlam, he had likened it to a surfacing whale, with the lesser hills as waves in that petrified sea.

This whale looked careworn. It bore quarry scars. Black Hole Quarry impresses by the scale of working – and by a surviving arch. The fell has heaps of displaced material where copper miners excavated levels while following the fickle veins. In his guide, AW had drawn some of the man-made entry points.

The first time I used an ice-axe for its intended purpose was on Wetherlam, yet there was little hint of arctic conditions as we parked near Tilberthwaite, in the tropical zone, and headed northwards with the tang of woodsmoke from a local farm to tickle our nostrils. The path, cut from the hillside, extended above the depths of Tilberthwaite Gill.

Last century, the hardiest of tourists had ventured there, attracted by the existence of wooded bridges that linked up paths as scary as goat-tracks. No bridges remain and walkers wisely keep to their high level route. In spring, I have heard the cool fluty whistle of a ring ouzel, which I think of as our northern nightingale.

The path which Bob and I followed led us through open country which that day was being over-run by the disciples of John Peel and their hounds. When the hunt had swept by, we meandered, then climbed with the bare bones of the landscape sticking out in lichened splendour. The haul to the skyline was unrelenting. The conditions became spartan. Came the moment when Bob fitted crampons to his boots and removed the protective piece of robber from the spike of his ice-axe prior to using it. Flexing his wrist, he advanced with a clumping gait.

It seemed over-dramatic until, on reaching the frozen, hail-sprinkled lower slope, I did a three-point landing, the third point being my head. Now the ice-axe was in use. With fresh confidence, and a mental image of Everest against which to act out my fantasies, I started to cut my staircase to heaven. Pausing for breath in the snowy conditions, my world shrunk by mist, I concentrated for a short time on action near at hand, such as the rate that hailstones were filling up the deep holes left by the shaft of Bob's ice-axe.

It was an anti-climax when we went over the rim and found the summit. We had another "Wainwright" to brag about and classified the climb as "hairy". The top of the fell had affinities with a skating rink. I resolved to return another day and look for yet another Lanty Slee's Cave. AW had marked this clearly. Lanty wanted a cave. He distilled whisky surreptitiously and needed somewhere to store it.

*Chapter Ten*

# The Latter Days – Haystacks with Ashes – Skiddaw Forest - Dear Betty – Milltown to Mountain.

The shy, red-haired lad who in his youth had responded to Alfred became a tall, well-padded, pipe-smoking man with a shock of silver-grey hair and mutton chop whiskers. He might be grumpy but through his books he endeared himself to a host of fellwalkers. In recent times, a series of television programmes, based on his Lakeland walks, and featuring Julia Bradbury, were issued - beamed to the nation at prime time as Wainwright Walks and subsequently issued as a DVD.

Towards the end of his life, the taciturn man of my early acquaintance bowed to the pressure of Media attention, granting interviews and allowing the BBC to make documentaries based on his books. The lone figure on the skyline who dodged behind rocks when he saw others approaching now had an audience numbered in millions.

Some people blamed him for the erosion of the fells caused by the pounding or slithering boots of a host of fell-walkers. When I broached the matter with him, he quietly replied that the invasion would have happened in any case. It was part of a resurgence of interest in the great outdoors. There is not much mention in his books of winter dangers. A friend comments that "quite a few of the routes described require an ice axe and preferably crampons in snow. Perhaps he kept to the lower ground in these conditions and expected that others would do the same."

The death of the Lancashire lad who became a Lakeland legend was attended by articles galore in newspapers and magazines. Richard North, Westmorland Gazette news editor: "The beauty of the books lies in their unique style and in Wainwright's unquenchable love for his subject." A H Griffin in The Guardian: "Once or twice I accompanied him on his walks, perhaps the only one of his friends who ever did so. Hills, for him, were places where a man should be by himself and he shunned the popular summits on crowded summer days, leaving their exploration to the winter time."

John Hillaby: "Towards the end of his life he went blind and lived in a mist. We prefer to think of the man who, unable to walk very far, sought slumber by retracing one of his favourite walks…"

The Dalesman: "Through his many distinctive books on our northern fell country, he had become something of a cult figure to countrygoers. Friends who have set themselves the task of doing 'all the Wainwrights' have had an absorbing hobby."

Eileen Jones, in the Yorkshire Post: "He loved maps and turned them into pictures, adding a human touch to the exactitude of the Ordnance Survey." Paul Wilson, under a heading, A Lakeland legend who changed my life: "There was no looking back for Wainwright. He abandoned all thought of climbing up the career ladder back in Blackburn: instead his sights were set on climbing the Lakeland hills, every one of them."

He had not seen anything beautiful in places of industrial dereliction, such as quarries and mines, but he visited them, moved by thoughts of generations of old-time workers. Had he not a faint memory of his upbringing in one of the busiest industrial towns of Lancashire? AW sensed that silence is always more profound in places that once were noisy. Using a six-inch map, he revelled in "the secret places that must be searched for".

He planned on his death to have his ashes scattered on Haystacks, in the western fells. To him, Haystacks was "the best fell-top of all, a place of great charm and fairytale attractiveness…" He concluded his Fellwanderers book with the now celebrated words: "And if you, dear reader, should get a bit of grit in your boot as you are crossing Haystacks in the years to come, please treat it with respect. It might be me." Bob lightly – and reverently – suggested that, with the average fell-walker, that bit of grit would end up on the floor of the local hostelry.

In my quest to stand on all the fells associated with the Wainwrights guides, I have especially fond memories of Great Calva, the nearest that a Lakeland fell comes to a pyramidic shape. By parking my car near Threlkeld I gained elevation and had an easy approach of about four miles, using the gap between Blencathra and Lonscale Fell.

I like Skiddaw Forest, a wild tract of land around the head of the infant River Caldew, because it is vast and sheep-speckled, with few human visitors, apart from those using a popular path to the summit of Skiddaw. On my latest visit, in a tardy springtime, I walked through a glorious alternation of sunny periods and showers of hail that periodically silvered the head of Skiddaw. The Weather Clerk gave a grim weather forecast, then swept the sky clear of cloud.

My path swerved, climbed and reached an elevation that provided a comfortable walk to Skiddaw House, a curious building, more like a terrace of houses than a single dwelling. AW might have seen affinities with the Lancashire housing of his childhood. Coronation Street in the wilderness. A solitary building, Skiddaw House was, when I visited it in 1993, possibly, the most remote dwelling in the Lake District. The resort

*Julia Bradbury braves the elements when shooting 'Coast to Coast'. (photo: Skyworks)*

*Over: BBC photograph of AW, issued at the time his walks were televised.*

of shepherds had become a Youth Hostel, offering a roof, bed and self-catering facilities.

When the sheep are not feeding on grass, they beg for sandwiches. At the time of my last visit, an unlocked door at the end of Skiddaw House led into a small bothy available to walkers at times when the hostel itself was not open. There was even a parcel containing a tin of soup and a bivvy bag. According to the warden, Skiddaw House had a ghost – that of Pearson Dalton, an old-time shepherd. Was this ghost story devised by the warden – an eerie story to relate as the hostellers prepared for bed? If, on their subsequent walking, they saw the old chap with his dog disappear through a wall, they shouldn't worry. He was "all right" and had just come back to have a look at the place.

My excursion to Great Calva continued using the track towards Dash Falls, from which I turned to go by peat and heather to the summit of my chosen fell – a summit plated with grey rock. From the top, Skiddaw House was the only building in sight over miles of open country. To the south, through the gap I had used on my inward journey, I could see as far as Thirlmere. It was a curious experience – almost like peering through a telescope being held the wrong way round.

The Blunderers found joy in their annual visit to the delightful Betty, whom AW first met in his Town Hall office in 1957; she had been summoned for a chat over the matter of an unpaid bill for a ballet company that had visited the town. Betty was born in Singapore, her father being a representative for a Lancashire cotton firm. She was well educated at Casterton, in the Lune Valley, and had taken courses in speech, drama and music. They fed her lively spirit.

Betty recalled her first sight of AW during the aforementioned visit to his tobacco-flavoured office at Kendal Town Hall. Seven years elapsed between that visit and the next meeting. Having bought one of his guide books, and being impressed by the art work, she sent what others might call a fan letter. In his turn, AW did not forget his meeting with Betty and especially her bright and positive manner. In a romantic mood, he compared the sight of her letter with a glimpse of the first primrose in springtime.

I visited Betty one November day, to get the dampness and chill out of my joints in her comfortable bungalow. She was in anecdotal mood, mentioning the time when AW and a BBC producer, while filming on the Northern Pennines, were approached by a rambler who asked: "Are you Mr Wainwright?" He replied, mischievously: "One

*BBC photograph of AW, issued at the time his walks were televised.*

*AW, photographed by Kenneth Shepherd on a pleasant walk from Kendal.*

of us is." Betty transformed AW's way of life. His reliance on smoking and fatty food, eaten at irregular times, had reduced him to such a poor state of health that hospitalisation was necessary.

He invited Betty to visit him for tea and talk. He also sent her a story he had written which purported to be fiction but, as he revealed, was autobiographical. It was of a man trapped in a loveless marriage who was exalted by thoughts of a dream lady. It is presumed that the loveless marriage was his. (Being a milltown lad, I have a soft spot for Ruth, whose early life was dominated by chapel and power looms.)

A note that accompanied AW's manuscript identified his dream lady as – Betty. She became his dream-wife. Both being divorcees, they were married in Kendal County Hall – not far from his old office, where they had first met - in March, 1970. AW was 63 years of age. They half-hoped for a marriage of ten years. In fact, they were wed for over twenty.

In Westmorland Heritage, AW paid warm tribute to the help he received from Betty. In compiling the book, she had not only done much research "but chauffered me over every road in the county and walked with me into the remotest corners; who has assisted me over stiles and gates (at which I was never adept), supplied sustenance, kept me buttoned up against the weather, guided my apprehensive steps in farmyards, and generally had sympathetic regard for my advanced years (without ever mentioning them, which would have annoyed me)."

Betty was the chauffeur when AW came to see me at my office in Clapham shortly before I retired. She announced that she would walk round the village. Would he be all right? AW, coming dangerously near smiling, said: "I think we'll find something to talk about." It crossed my mind that at my first meeting with Wainwright, he had been in the seat at the desk; now I had that distinction. He was the visitor.

I suggested we might have a bar snack at The Gamecock in Austwick. Betty readily agreed. AW was not so sure. In the end, we had the bar snack. Betty drove us to the next village using what – her driving style being jerky – I fancifully thought of as kangaroo petrol. Betty and I ate well. AW was not especially hungry except for the fumes from his pipe. We chatted with others, outdoors, in the sunshine before the return journey began. Were the villagers aware that here was a man who had created the classic seven walking guides to the Lake District fells – and over 50 other books.

The car was driven jerkily along the Clapham by-pass, from which there are three

*Betty and AW during a visit to Cumbria magazine at Clapham.*

roads leading into the village. I suggested to Betty that she might drop me off so I could walk back to the office. When I waved them off, Betty was at the wheel and AW's head and shoulders were framed by the back window. He detested wearing a seat-belt, which at that time was obligatory only to those sitting in a front seat. It began to rain. I had no way of avoiding getting soaked before I was back at the office.

AW was undoubtedly a character – a person with a distinctive way of looking at the world. In his writing, he was perceptive, helpful and entertaining. Compiling the Guides was that old-fashioned occupation – a labour of love. When the Geriatric Blunders, disciples of AW, climbed Great End in ice and snow, it was a day in a thousand with a northerly breeze to provide clarity. The sharpness of the horizons and the fine detail of the crags and gullies were like lines on a Wainwright drawing.

He met a woman suffering from depression who, uplifted by his books, had climbed Scafell. Said AW: "The fells are a marvellous tonic. There is no doubt they can help people. I have never felt 'down' or depressed when I have been up there." In my book After You, Mr Wainwright, published in 1992 and dedicated to Betty, I listed his chief likes and dislikes.

LIKES: Betty, Skylines, Pipe and Tobacco, Fish and Chips, Maps, Well-used Boots, Blackburn Rovers, Coronation Street, Old Kendal, Cats (not so keen on dogs), Yet More Fish and Chips. DISLIKES: Gaelic Names for Scottish Mountains, Sociable Fell-walkers, Passing the time of day with School Parties (one "good morning" had to do), Car Seat Belts, Cruelty to Animals, Bad Grammar, Most places South of Blackburn.

Came the day, in January, 1991, when Alfred Wainwright, MBE, departed this mortal life, aged eighty-four. He was in hospital at the time of his death and Betty was at his side. He had written, on the last page of the seventh Lakeland guide: "The fleeting hour of life of those who love the hills is quickly spent, but the hills are eternal."

I recalled sidelights of his life. AW was in some respects like his fellow Lancashireman, the artist Lowry. Both could be irascible and both cherished privacy, as evidence by their work. Whereas Lowry might draw the odd "matchstick dog" to go with his "matchstick men", AW often portrayed sheep. He had no profound knowledge of natural history. The golden eagle he drew for Riggindale looks like a barnyard fowl.

Arthur Ransome, author of classic children's stories with Lakeland settings, transformed Coniston Old Man into Kanchenjunga. To Wainwright, this immense fell was the Matterhorn, with the village of Coniston as the Lakeland equivalent of Zermatt. AW died without climbing over the Lion's Mane on Helm Crag, above Grasmere.

He must have felt frustrated, though he did not have the figure for rock-climbing and he acknowledged that this is one of the very few summits in Lakeland reached by climbing rocks. On the page in his pictorial guide relating to the view from Helm Crag, AW left a postage-stamp-sized space for an announcement that he had succeeded in surmounting the highest point. In the first edition, he wrote somewhat glumly: "Up to the time of going to press, however, such an announcement cannot be made."

AW was not over-sensitive about sticking to rights of way. One recommended route crossed a prime and much cherished grouse moor. AW was aware of the very special – very private – status of The Nab, at the heart of the Martindale Deer Forest. He mentioned the "keep out" notices, the barricaded gates and barbed wire that even the dullest of walkers would recognise as a deterrent.

He attained the grassy summit of the fell, of course, acknowledging in the appropriate pictorial guide that he had trespassed. (He did not write for permission to climb the Nab through a fear of being refused!) He sneaked in and was undetected possibly, as he wrote, because of his marked resemblance to an old stag!

At his request, he was cremated. Early on a bright morning, Betty scattered the ashes on Haystacks, which AW affirmed had "the best fell-top of all" and where he wished his remains to repose. Haystacks was AW's last peak by dint not only of the ash-scattering but because, not long before, he had been taken there by the BBC for a film. It was a chilling, wet day. "The mountains wept for me that day; it never stopped raining."

He had always fancied Haystacks while admitting it was not much to brag about. It sits "unabashed and unashamed in the midst of a circle of much loftier fells, like a shaggy terrier in the company of foxhounds." Elsewhere, he described it as the best fell-top of all, "a place of great charm and fairy tale attractiveness..."

Visiting Innominate Tarn, on Haystacks, is the nearest I have come to a Cumbrian pilgrimage. AW would have been somewhat embarrassed could he have known that I would use such a term. He was not a religious person, despite the grandeur of the Lakeland landscape, which has induced religious thoughts in many another.

On my most recent visit to Haystacks, I did not make his favourite approach, from Buttermere village, following the lakeshore before the climb began. From this direction, soaring crags give the impression that Haystacks is much taller than it actually is. The name is said to be derived from the Norse name for High Rocks. The romantic imagines the scattered tors are Haystacks, being like stacks of hay in a summer meadow.

I approached AW's last resting place from Ennerdale, breaking tree cover to find myself on a sun-baked hillside littered with stones that clacked and clinked at every footfall.

The view had opened out. Pillar rose ponderously across the dale. Ennerdale Water, in the lower part of the valley, and away to the west, was a Mediterranean blue. Before I stormed Haystacks' cliffbound rim, I looked down, down, down into the Buttermere valley, with its trilogy of lovely lakes. I glanced across to Grasmoor, a mighty fell which, this day, had been cut down to size by cloud.

Wainwright was on my mind. Friends who wanted to raise a simple felltop memorial had been battling for four years with planners who now had rejected several suggested sites. Joyfully I heard that an idea to re-name Innominate Tarn (which means "nameless") after AW had been turned down. In a recent issue of The Westmorland Gazette I read some letters from readers who were objecting to a proposal to erect a statue of AW at Kendal. He would surely have been agin the idea.

When I reached the Haystacks plateau, I walked through a familiar labyrinth of rocks, knolls, tarns, cracks, crevices and coarse vegetation. On the relatively dry parts, heather bloomed, bees droned from flower to flower, and bilberries yielded lustrous fruit for the fell-going birds to pick. The tarns, in their peaty hollows, were flanked by cotton grass and sphagnun moss. Innominate Tarn, as I now saw it, was flecked with silver and stirred by a light easterly wind.

There is a modest memorial to AW in Buttermere Church. It is an inscribed piece of slate, on a window sill, leaving space for a vase of flowers. In good weather, the view through the window is of upsweeping crags – AW's "wall of defending crags" – rising precipitously from Warnscale Bottom to Haystacks.

In a long lifetime, AW came a long way from a modest terraced house in a poverty-stricken but law-abiding milltown with a forest of smoking chimneys. In his young days, he bathed in a zinc bath before an open fire that was set between an iron oven and boiler. These were kept clean by applications of black-lead.

He had seen the ritual of lighting and extinguishing a gaslight. He watched his ever-busy mother lowering and raising a wooden rack on which the clothes she had laboriously washed were aired. And, of course, this Lancashire family had an aspidistra. His earliest hill-walking was on "tops" within viewing distance of milldom – among them Longridge Fell and Pendle Hill.

AW's fame led to the name Wainwright being associated with a bridge, a shire horse and even a brand of beer. The next major topic along these lines was a proposal by Kendal council to spend £80,000 on a bronze statue of the reclusive man. It would be set up at Kendal. The chosen designer had provided the figure of Eric Morecambe for Morecambe seafront and also a statue of Laurel and Hardy in Ulverston. AW had made it clear to relatives and friends that he did not want to be commemorated by a statue.

*Stan and Colin by the tarn on Haystacks.*

After his death, and when living in a large bungalow at Burneside, Betty followed the activities of our little Blunderers' group, receiving reports – and later, from Bob, tape recordings of reports – relating to our fortnightly sorties into Wainwright Country. (AW would scarcely have approved of our tongue-in-cheek motto: "You name it, we've been lost on it.") On a particularly wet day, Betty allowed me to put my sodden notes of our latest expedition in her oven, specially heated, so that the record of our excursion would dry before degenerating into mush.

On his death, our friendship with Betty endured, to the end. She had a stroke in 2004 and made a slight recovery. Betty found the Blunderers' report headed Hills of Sheep "very entertaining". Bob and myself were the sheep-spotters. The Big Country theme had come to mind as we left the M6 for a web of narrow roads around the village of Great Asby.

At first we were on strips of tarmac laid on open ground, with a few flanking posts to indicate the way after dark or at snowtime. The countryside undulated, not quite tickling the 1,000-ft contour. Most of the hills had grey pates [limestone outcrops]. There was a scattering of sheep and piebald ponies, the last-named being helpfully conspicuous to speeding motorists.

At Great Asby, tethered goats on the green did not even bother to look up from their grazing as we went by. The road was fringed by clumps of daffodils. Local names for buildings fascinated us. There was Great Kettle Barn and Pate Hole Mouth. Beyond the village, a buzzard circled. At a croakery (a small boy's name for a rookery) the early squabbling over nesting sites was over. The birds had settled down to a low-pitched cawing. Curlews were trilling    sounds that stirred some life into mist as damp as a dish-clout [cloth].

These were, indeed, hills of sheep. Hills well-known to AW. He did not seek company but must have enjoyed meeting the occasional characterful local farmer, such as the man Bob and I met. He kept three unusual types of sheep – Jacob's (them wi' horns), Leicester (straight up and down) and Texel (big-arsed)!

We used stiles and gates in our fairly rapid progress across country. A middle-aged jogger who passed us, with a spaniel in tow, had bare feet. On rougher ground, where limestone outcropped, we used map, compass and a newspaper cutting from the Westmorland Gazette to fix our position.

Beyond Sunbiggin we took to the hill country – to a sweeping landscape of meadows and pastures, a pattern of limestone walls and, beyond, open fell with yet another crust of grey outcrops. On the open common were sheep distinguished by having a red blob on the nape and blue blob on the body.

So we reached Great Asby Scar (prop: English Nature) where three taciturn wallers were repairing a big gap to ensure that sheep could not enter what was conspicuously sheep-ravaged country, thatched with tracts of Nardus stricta, or "bent", which developed after the previous vegetation was desecrated by too many champing sheep.

Wainwright was dead – but his spirit lived on. During an October day in 2006, we three – Bob, Colin and I – ascended Pendle Hill, which to the rambler is hallowed ground. It was hereabouts that AW, as a Blackburn lad, had his baptism of hill-walking. From the Hill, he would see the verdant Ribble Valley to the north and, elsewhere, smudges of smoke lingering over the East Lancashire milltowns.

Bob had chosen to climb Pendle because he was familiar with the Hill. He saw it through the kitchen window at his home in Settle while washing-up after a meal. I was delighted to take part in the ascent, having ventured on to Pendle many times, originally prompted by the book Mist over Pendle. When I interviewed Robert Neill, the author, who retired to Keswick, he told me he had written the book during an otherwise boring spell of naval service on the Northern Isles of Scotland. (Though it was largely a work of imagination, a Lancashire bookseller would not take on any copies until he had been out and about on his bike to check the accuracy of the text!)

Calling ourselves Pendalians, we set off on the first day of December, 2004, approaching a mist-capped Pendle from the car park at Barley. Soon we were sauntering in an area where gills are cloughs and becks have become brooks. Bob directed us to the Pendle Hill Circular Walk, the start of which was indicated by large painted signs.

Colin recalled that when he last climbed the Hill he met a man who was digging a hole atoppe of ye mountain (as George Fox, a notable Quaker visitor, might have written). The old man dropped a dead dog into the hole, remarking that the animal had often been to the hilltop with him. It was a fitting place for its burial.

The path that runs diagonally up the side of the Hill was paved and stepped. We found a level spot for our first (minor) buttying-place. As we traversed the summit plateau of Pendle, we were buzzed by a helicopter. What would AW have written about that? Being isolated, Pendle in winter is shiveringly cold. (I prefer Maytime, when heather on the summit plateau is sprouting green. At that time, a trip of dotterels, rare passage migrants, breaks a journey on their way from winter quarters by the Mediterranean to wild northern lands, including the Cairngorms in Scotland.)

AW was familiar with a boggy route westwards and a descent into a large clough in which the beck has an attractive series of ox-bows and there are two reservoirs. Walls – standard in appearance - follow the contours like stretches of Hadrian's Wall, being attractively castellated by stones of uniform size. It was mating time on the "Hills of Sheep". Most of the Swaledale yows [ewes] had blue rumps, the dye transferred from an amorous tup to confirm its mating success.

*Wintering sheep seeking fodder on the eastern fells.*

AW must have known Pendle when mist was so thick you might almost taste it. On another day, when our intention was to complete the 40-mile Pendle Way, a curtain of mist had fallen on the old hill. It was not just a matter of Mist Over Pendle but Mist All Over Pendle. We were uncertain we had climbed it until we stubbed our toes on a mist-shrouded trig point at just short of 2,000-ft.

From Newchurch, we had climbed using compass readings in the mist. Beyond a stile was a path that led us ultimately on to a man-made path through a gloomy conifer wood. Steps had been laid to ease the descent to Lower Ogden reservoir – the water Bob and I had seen on the previous Pendle outing. This time, the Weather Clerk turned on a celestial tap. Rain beat a tattoo against our waterproof clothes.

With a choice of paths, and mist still dense, we began a steady climb, slithering on dark peat and scrambling across lively, peat-stained becks topped by swirling cream-coloured suds. Colin shouted: "It's levelling out." We laughed immoderately. Colin had decided that we must walk on a line of 300 degrees. Or thereabouts. We were now in virgin territory. A sheep looked startled. A solitary grouse departed, fast and low, chuckling at our plight.

Working on the principal that because Pendle Hill was isolated, all we had to do was maintain an upward course to find ourselves at the summit. So we followed the murky figure of Colin, who frequently consulted his map. We did not actually see him shake the compass. A chilly wind blew from the south-east.

A smile drifted across Colin's face as he pointed to the ground, where there were unmistakeable signs of a footpath. Marker cairns appeared to view and – hurrah – we found the trig point, Number 2161, as the meticulous AW would have noted if he had being climbing Pendle. Ten minutes later, the mist began to rise like a curtain at a pantomime.

Looking south, as AW had done in his young days, we could now trace most of the course of the Pendle Way. As we negotiated a footpath to Barley, one of two young men, commenting on the improvement in the weather, said: "T'sun's rays'll be cracking flagstones in an hour."

Betty lived long enough to be able to listen to our Pendle excursion. When the Blunderers last met her, she was a wisp of a lady, with snow-white hair. Spirited, adroitly using a walking aid on wheels, she promptly led us on a garden tour. Betty died at the age of 86. The Blunderers were in the congregation at a commemorative service in Burneside Church.

Martin Wainwright, in his Guardian obituary, had written of her: "She had a twinkle which awoke the counterpart in Wainwright, a sense of fun long-suppressed by his...solitary treks on the hills."

Eric Robson, in an anecdotal address, mentioned Betty's driving. At some event, she had got into a field. He said: "She was the only person I knew who had done a 13 point turn to get out." Betty's only fault was her driving. It was quite hairy. And it's perhaps fortunate that his eyesight was going in those latter days."

Those of us fortunate enough to have known AW as a friend are conscious that he transformed our way of looking at the fell-country. By encouraging us to get up and walk – to get to the top! – he prolonged our active lives. On the Blunderer's last visit to President Betty, not long before her death, we were surprised when she set off from the house with her three-wheeler, keen to show us the large garden, which was in an immaculate state.

We insisted on making afternoon tea, which was a single course – toast. With four men involved, the results were surprisingly varied and Bob, who operated the toaster, had scorched fingers. Betty was amused at the tonal range of the toast – from ginger to ember. Bob described Betty as "a lovely lady, very much the power behind the throne and having but one weakness, to which Eric Robson had so astutely alluded. It was to do with her car driving." But then, as Bob says – nobody's perfect.

*At home with Betty Wainwright.*

*Family members outside AW's birthplace when a plaque in his memory was unveiled.*

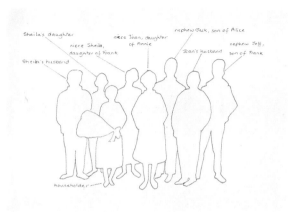

*Epilogue*

# When Eyes Are Dimmed.

In April, 1988, Dorothy Hemsworth sent a copy of a poem (author unknown) to AW having heard of the decline in his eyesight:

*When the days come that I must live alone*
*In my thoughts, and when my eyes are dimmed*
*And cannot see the shadows on the hills*
*Cast by the clouds, and when I cannot hear*
*The far-off sounds of hurrying streams and sheep –*
*Then I will turn my mind to those great days*
*I spent upon the fells, and I will count them over, one by one.*
*I will remember rain and bitter winds,*
*The feel of clothes drenched by stinging showers;*
*Tea at a wayside inn with some good friends,*
*Hot baths and fires, warmth for tired limbs,*
*And all the liveliness of home and rest.*

*And while I think of all those joyous days,*
*Of all the heights I've gained, hours I've lived,*
*I will not envy those who take their turn*
*In tramping manfully in storm or fine*
*The hills I knew, for they are part of me –*
*A heritage of beauty nought can spoil.*

AW replied: "It is always a pleasure to hear from others who share my love of the Lakeland fells and northern hills, as you so obviously do…The lovely poem expresses my own feelings and sentiments so well. I will treasure this."

*Also by W.R. Mitchell, available from Great Northern Books:*

## HANNAH HAUXWELL – 80 Years in the Dales

*The Official Biography to Celebrate the 80th Birthday of this Remarkable Dales Character*
Hannah captured the hearts of the nation when she was the subject of an
extraordinary documentary, *Too Long a Winter*. The TV programme made her a
national celebrity. Further programmes followed. She went on tours of Europe and
America, shook hands with the Pope and played the piano on the Orient Express.
This major book traces the extraordinary life of a delightful personality who has
never lost her links with the dales countryside. It includes many previously
unpublished photographs.
*Fully illustrated. Hardback.*

## THUNDER IN THE MOUNTAINS
## The Men Who Built Ribblehead

For years the dominant sounds at Ribblehead were the bleating of sheep and the
croaky calls of grouse. Then came the railway engineers and their men, linking Settle
with Carlisle. Thunderous noises, including a new-fangled explosive called dynamite,
echoed in and around the mountains. Ribblehead Viaduct, which symbolises the
strength and durability of the Settle-Carlisle railway, was built by a Victorian work
force. How that force was mustered, and how its various skills were applied in a bleak
high Pennine setting, are related in this beautifully produced and fully illustrated
hardback. The railway settlement on and around Batty Green, at the headwaters of
the Ribble, lived, throve and died in less than ten years. The workforce, their wives
and children, experienced earthquake, flood and an outbreak of smallpox. As men
constructed the longest viaduct on the line, others were hacking and blasting their
way through Blea Moor, warming dynamite in their pockets before use!
As befits the twentieth anniversary of saving the Settle- Carlisle railway from
closure, a final chapter brings the Ribblehead story up-to-date. It looks at how the
saga turned full circle and a temporary settlement again appeared at Ribblehead to
see through a massive rebuild of the aging structure.
*Fully illustrated. Hardback.*

*Visit www.greatnorthernbooks.co.uk*